CULTURE SMART!
INDONESIA

Graham Saunders

·K·U·P·E·R·A·R·D·

First published in Great Britain 2007
by Kuperard, an imprint of Bravo Ltd
59 Hutton Grove, London N12 8DS
Tel: +44 (0) 20 8446 2440 Fax: +44 (0) 20 8446 2441
www.culturesmartguides.com
Inquiries: sales@kuperard.co.uk

Culture Smart! is a registered trademark of Bravo Ltd

Distributed in the United States and Canada
by Random House Distribution Services
1745 Broadway, New York, NY 10019
Tel: +1 (212) 572-2844 Fax: +1 (212) 572-4961
Inquiries: csorders@randomhouse.com

Copyright © 2007 Kuperard

Revised 2008; second printing

Series Editor Geoffrey Chesler
Design Bobby Birchall

ISBN 978 1 85733 343 5

British Library Cataloguing in Publication Data
A CIP catalogue entry for this book is available from the
British Library

Printed in Malaysia

Cover image: Fishing boat on Kanawa Island, Nusa Tenggara. *Travel-Ink/Patrick Ford*
The photographs on pages 85, 125 and 127 are reproduced by permission of the author.

About the Author

GRAHAM SAUNDERS has a Ph.D in East Asian studies from the University of Hull, England. An Australian by birth, he spent twenty-eight years teaching in East Malaysia and Brunei, and has made numerous visits to the countries of the region, including Indonesia. He then taught in Cyprus for five years before he and his wife, Anne, settled in England near York. After some part-time university lecturing he retired to run a business specializing in books on Southeast Asia. He is the author of a number of books and articles on the history of Borneo and Southeast Asia.

The Culture Smart! series is continuing to expand.
For further information and latest titles visit
www.culturesmartguides.com

The publishers would like to thank **CultureSmart!**Consulting for its help in researching and developing the concept for this series.

CultureSmart!Consulting creates tailor-made seminars and consultancy programs to meet a wide range of corporate, public-sector, and individual needs. Whether delivering courses on multicultural team building in the USA, preparing Chinese engineers for a posting in Europe, training call-center staff in India, or raising the awareness of police forces to the needs of diverse ethnic communities, it provides essential, practical, and powerful skills worldwide to an increasingly international workforce.

For details, visit www.culturesmartconsulting.com

CultureSmart!Consulting and **CultureSmart!** guides have both contributed to and featured regularly in the weekly travel program "Fast Track" on BBC World TV.

contents

contents

Map of Indonesia

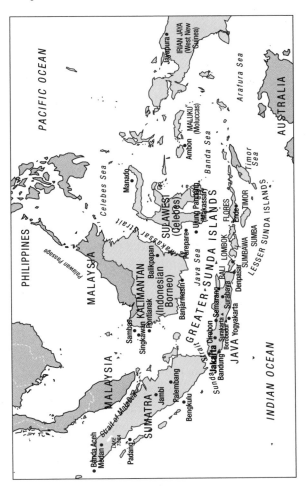

introduction

Indonesia is the world's largest archipelago. With a population of more than 200 million, it is the fifth most populous country in the world. Its position on the trade routes has produced a rich and diverse culture influenced by animist, Hindu, Buddhist, Christian, and Muslim traditions. The capital, Jakarta, is a teeming megalopolis whose central business and financial district has all the trappings of twenty-first century global enterprise, but whose culture does not necessarily conform to that of the U.S.A. and Europe.

Although European influence began to penetrate the archipelago in the sixteenth century, Dutch colonialism gained full political control over most of the country only in the nineteenth century. From Batavia (Jakarta) the Dutch dominated Java, but their influence in the outer islands was patchy. Consequently, the nationalist movement of the twentieth century was mainly Java-centered. Although Indonesian nationalism was largely secular, Islam retained and continues to have great influence, though filtered through other traditional cultural prisms; Bali remains Hindu, and Christianity is strong in Ambon and also in Minahasa, in northern Sulawesi. European influence is just one element in the cultural blend.

There are some three hundred ethnic groups in Indonesia, the product of centuries of migration and settlement. The differences between ethnic groups and social classes are clearly understood, but underlying this diversity, and the more recent cultural impact of the West, are common core values. The apparently modern and Westernized Indonesian lives according to beliefs and perceptions that the visitor needs to be aware of in order not to offend unintentionally: the principles of social conduct reflect an Asian approach to the world. These values lie deep, and influence behavior that to outsiders may seem irrational or perplexing while statements, gestures, or other conduct perfectly natural to the visitor may produce adverse reactions from Indonesians. In general, though, Indonesians are gracious and will make allowances for strangers.

Culture Smart! Indonesia provides an introduction to this rich diversity while enabling you to avoid some of the social pitfalls when visiting, living, or working in this fascinating and beautiful country. Indonesians are a hospitable and courteous people. By making an effort to understand and respect their values and customs, you will earn their appreciation and friendship.

Key Facts

Official Name	Republik Indonesia (Republic of Indonesia)	
Capital City	Jakarta	Pop. 9.3 million
Major Cities	Bandung; Cirebon; Semarang; Surabaya; Yogyakarta (Java). Denpasar (Bali). Mataram (Lombok). Medan; Padang; Jambi; Palembang (Sumatra). Pontianak; Banjarmasin; Balikpapan (Kalimantan). Ujung Pandang; Manado (Sulawesi). Ambon (Maluku); Jayapura (Irian Jaya)	
Main Island Groups	Greater Sunda Islands: Sumatra, Java, Kalimantan (Indonesian Borneo), Sulawesi (Celebes) Lesser Sunda Islands (Nusa Tenggara): Bali, Lombok, Sumbawa, Komodo, Sumba, Flores, Timor, Alor Also: Maluku (the Moluccas), Irian Jaya (West New Guinea)	
Area	742,308 sq. miles (1,919,440 sq. km)	17,508 islands, 6,000 inhabited
Climate	Tropical. Hot and humid; more moderate in highlands	Coastal temp. range is 70–91°F (21–33°C) throughout year
Currency	Indonesian rupiah	Approx. Rp 9,700 = U.S. $1 (2005)
Population	245 million	Current rowth rate 1.41% per annum (2006 est.)
Ethnic Makeup	Javanese 45% Sundanese 14% Madurese 7.5% Coastal Malays 7.5 % Other 26%	
Age Structure	0–14 years: 28.8% 15–64 years: 65.8% 65+ years: 5.4%	

Language	Bahasa Indonesia (official form of Malay)	300 regional languages and dialects, with Javanese the most widespread, plus English and Dutch
Adult Literacy	Approx. 87% over age 15 (2002 est.)	Male: 92.5%. Female: 83.4%
Religion	Muslim 88%; Christian 8% (Protestant 5%, Catholic 3%); Hindu 2%; Buddhist 1%; animist 1%	Belief in God is a tenet of the Pancasila—The Five Principles of the State.
Government	Federal Republic. The President, elected for five years, is both Head of State and Head of Government.	Unicameral House of Representatives, or Dewan Perwakilan Rakyat (DPR), elected for five years. Voting age is 17 years
Media	TV and radio in Bahasa Indonesia. English-language media via satellite	Newspapers in Bahasa Indonesia and in English
Electricity	220 volts, 50 Hz	Plugs are 2-pin. Adaptors available
Telephone	Indonesia's country code is 62.	The code for Jakarta is 62 21.
TV/Video	PAL system	Compatible with U.K.
Time Zones	Indonesia has three Standard Time zones: Western (GMT + 7 hrs.), Central (GMT + 8 hrs.), and Eastern (GMT + 9 hrs.).	

chapter one

LAND & PEOPLE

GEOGRAPHY

Indonesia is the world's largest island nation, consisting of more than 17,000 islands stretching 3,200 miles (5,000 km) from the northern tip of Sumatra to Irian Jaya in West New Guinea. It occupies a strategic position between Asia and Australia, and between the Indian Ocean and the Pacific, straddling the main sea route between India and Europe to the west and China and Japan to the east. For centuries, control of the Malacca Strait between Sumatra and the Malayan peninsula on the one hand and of the Sunda Strait separating Sumatra and Java on the other, and of the Palawan passage between Borneo and the southern Philippines, enabled powerful and wealthy maritime kingdoms to emerge.

Indonesia has more than six thousand inhabited islands, which geographers have placed in three main groups. The large islands of Sumatra, Java, Kalimantan (Indonesian Borneo), and Sulawesi (Celebes) comprise the group known as the Greater Sundas. The chain of smaller islands east of

Java, from Bali through Lombok, Sumbawa, Sumba, and Flores to Timor, comprise the Lesser Sundas. Known as Nusa Tenggara, they are divided into West Nusa Tenggara (Bali, Lombok) and East Nusa Tenggara. The third region, east of Sulawesi and north of the Lesser Sundas, is the Moluccas (Maluku). Irian Jaya, as part of the large island of New Guinea, is a distinctive region in its own right.

Indonesia stretches across three time zones: Western, Central, and Eastern Indonesian Standard Time (GMT + 7 hours to GMT + 9 hours).

Some 70 percent of the population live on Java, an island about the size of England. Java has a volcanic spine and fertile volcanic soils producing coffee, sugar, and rice. In historical terms, the intensive rice culture of central Java supported substantial Hindu and Buddhist kingdoms, which have left significant architectural remains similar to those found on the mainland of Southeast Asia.

Elsewhere, maritime trading kingdoms dominated the sea-lanes. These included Srivijaya, which for centuries controlled both the Malacca and Sunda Straits from its capital at Palembang on the east coat of Sumatra. Further north, Aceh, from its position on the north coast of Sumatra, in the fourteenth century commanded the northern approach to the Malacca Strait. Its early conversion to Islam was a testament to its importance for Arab and Indian Muslim traders.

On the east coast of Java various port kingdoms contested the Sunda Strait, with Majapahit acquiring prominence in the fourteenth century, remembered in Javanese tradition as a golden age. Similar maritime empires rose and fell over time, many of them leaving little in permanent remains as their defenses were their ships, and their conquests trade and influence rather than land. They also lacked the large peasant populations that provided the labor for building the temples of central Java. Nevertheless, the Bugis of Makassar in southern Sulawesi are still renowned for their prowess as seafarers. Finally, the islands were to fall under the aegis of another maritime trading power, the Dutch.

This mercantile history was determined by the geographical nature of the region that became Indonesia. It was easier to travel across the sea than to cross the mountainous interiors of most of the islands. The sea linked the region rather than separated it, and created a pattern of development that was largely coastal. The main exception was Java, with its rich volcanic soils, a factor also in supporting Bali's population. The sea continues to bind the nation together, although now supplemented by air travel. Moreover, modern road and river transportation has improved access to the interior of the various islands, while modern communications have made easier the inculcation of an Indonesian identity. Nevertheless, the particular regional cultures, which make Indonesia such a fascinating and diverse country, continue to be largely protected by the geographical factors that have shaped the region for centuries.

CLIMATE

The climate is tropical with a wet and a dry season, although in many regions the latter is in fact a less wet season. Day temperatures at sea level rise to 76–85°F (26–30°C) throughout the year and it is generally hot and humid. The evenings are pleasantly warm. Jakarta is generally hotter and more uncomfortable than the other main cities. Temperatures become cooler in the mountains. November to April is generally the rainy season and May to October is relatively dry. This pattern is reversed for Sumatra and central Maluku. There are also local variations caused by local geographical factors. Straddling the equator, the country has little seasonal variation in the lengths of day and night.

On the whole, it is a climate suited to activity in the morning and evenings and a siesta in the afternoon. In practice, offices and businesses keep going with electric fans and air-conditioning.

ENVIRONMENT

The most significant environmental concerns relate to the impact of inadequately controlled logging, particularly in East Kalimantan and southern Sumatra. In recent years, during the dry season, smoke from forest fires has created atmospheric haze, which has also affected in particular East Malaysia, Brunei, Singapore, and West Malaysia. Logging has also led to the leaching and loss of topsoil and to the pollution of rivers with detrimental effects upon fish stocks. The government has difficulty in imposing its authority over the logging companies. Generally speaking, environmental controls are rarely properly enforced. As the effects of environmental degradation become more widely felt, however, the situation is being taken more seriously.

This is also true of the maritime environment, which has suffered from illegal fishing techniques, leading to damaged coral reefs. Again, regulations are often difficult to enforce. The natural environment is one of Indonesia's greatest assets, however. The beaches and coral reefs provide opportunities for scuba diving, snorkeling, and other activities. Spectacular coastal and mountain scenery attracts tourists who want merely to view and those who seek more adventure. With this, the landscape and forests have acquired a new commercial importance and there is a growing awareness that conservation is an important contributor to the local and national economy. Events of recent years have highlighted the importance of tourism; the need to diversify this sector and to protect Indonesia's natural assets is being recognized.

Indonesia has signed numerous international agreements relating to climate change and environmental issues. It is a signatory to the Kyoto Protocol and to other agreements relating to the protection of the ozone layer, biodiversity, endangered species, the conservation of tropical timbers, the preservation of wetlands, and pollution controls. This environmental concern holds hope for more effective action.

NATURAL DISASTERS

Indonesia comprises part of the Pacific "Ring of Fire" and over time has suffered major volcanic eruptions. Many of its natural features are the products of volcanic activity, among them Lake Toba (Sumatra), Mount Batur (Bali), and Mount Rinjani (Lombok), each with its crater lake. The largest eruption in modern times was that of the island of Krakatau, blasted apart in 1883 and now re-forming. Even greater was that of Mount Tambura on Sumbawa in 1815; more recently, in 1982, Mount Galumggung erupted. Over seventy volcanoes remain active.

The province of Aceh in North Sumatra suffered seriously from the tsunami of December 2004. In addition there are the threats of flooding and landslides from heavy rainfall, especially in areas where deforestation has occurred.

A BRIEF HISTORY

Modern Indonesia is the product of a long and complex history. Hominid remains found in Java have been dated to some one million years ago. "Java Man," discovered in 1890, is recognized as a member of the species *Homo erectus*, the precursor of modern man, and large numbers of stone tools dating from between 500,000 and 250,000 years ago have been found in eastern Java. *Homo sapiens* appeared in the region about 50,000 years ago. These have been identified as Austronesians, who from about 5000 BCE were gradually displaced or absorbed by Mongolian migrations from mainland Asia. Stone tools became increasingly refined. Animals were domesticated, food crops (particularly taro, a root crop) cultivated, and village communities established. Pottery and megalithic monuments provide evidence of a flourishing Neolithic culture. Trade developed between islands and with mainland Southeast Asia.

From around 500 BCE the Dong-son bronze culture of northern Vietnam spread to Indonesia, as did rice cultivation. Chinese records mention the eastern islands of the archipelago as sources of cloves and it is clear that a system of trade had developed. Not all areas of Indonesia

were equally affected and Neolithic practices continued in some isolated areas until recent times, but Indonesia was taking on its distinctive character.

Trade and Kingdoms

Sophisticated states began to emerge in Southeast Asia in the second century CE, by which time trade links had extended westward. These states were profoundly influenced by India and were, at first, Hindu and, later, Buddhist. On Sumatra, the great trading empire of Srivijaya lasted for several centuries but left no major monuments, perhaps because it had no large peasant population to call upon for labor. On Java, agriculture flourished on the volcanic soils and several states rose and fell, the ruins of great temples and monuments testifying to their wealth and power. The Buddhist Sailendra rulers of central Java, who built Borobudur, were succeeded by Hindu dynasties, culminating in the fourteenth-century empire of Majapahit, which embraced much of the archipelago. In the fifteenth century, establishing itself first in Aceh, Muslim influence greatly increased and eventually dominated the islands, only Bali holding out. Throughout the archipelago sultanates were established that retained most of the traditional government structures from the pre-Islamic past. The existing court ceremonies were adapted, not abolished. The underlying pre-Islamic culture remained largely unaffected, particularly on Java.

Dutch Colonialism

By the beginning of the sixteenth century the Portuguese had entered the region and soon established themselves at Malacca and in the spice islands of the Moluccas (Maluku). The Dutch and English followed in the seventeenth century, the Dutch establishing themselves at Batavia (Jakarta) and eventually excluding the English, though the English East India Company clung on to Bengkulan (Benkulu) in southwest Sumatra until 1824, when they settled all their territorial disputes in the region with the Dutch. The Dutch East India Company (known by its initials V.O.C.) extended its influence much in the manner of its traditional predecessors, concentrating on trade rather than conquest. For a brief period, 1811–16, during the Napoleonic Wars, the English returned to Batavia. It was during this time that Thomas Stamford Raffles, the eventual founder of Singapore, wrote his acclaimed *History of Java*.

Once reestablished in Batavia, the Dutch began to extend their control over the Javanese sultanates and to encourage agriculture for export. With the development of steam power and, after 1850, growing demand in Europe for tropical products, and to forestall revived British interest in the region, the Dutch extended their claims to the whole archipelago, which became the Dutch East Indies. They met prolonged resistance in Aceh, which they defeated in 1908 (although Aceh remained under martial law until 1918). The Portuguese retained a toehold in East Timor and the British on the northwest coast of Borneo and in Papua. The political boundaries of what became Indonesia were thereby set.

Indonesian Nationalism

Indonesian nationalism developed in the early years of the nineteenth century. Some knowledge of its history is necessary because it still resonates with Indonesians today. Its beginnings were cultural rather than openly political, and its origins are traced back to the writings of a young woman, Raden Adjeng Kartini, born into an aristocratic family, who is commemorated on April 21 each year with a national public holiday, Kartini Day. Her concerns were to encourage the education of girls and to raise the status of Indonesian women. She lived only to the age of twenty-five, but she inspired others to take up the cause of education, particularly Dr. Mas Wahidin Sudiro Husudo, who prompted a group of young medical students to establish the Budi Utomo (Noble Endeavor) organization in Batavia on May 20, 1908. Dutch policy at the time was to supply village education, but the villagers had first to build their own schools. Budi Utomo members toured villages in Java to encourage this effort, which expanded into promotion of other forms of social and cultural improvement.

In 1911, another strand of national feeling emerged when the Sarekat Dagang Islam (Islamic Traders' Association) was formed by Hadji Samanhudi of Surakarta to organize Javanese batik traders facing competition from the Chinese by forming cooperative societies. In 1913, the name was changed to Sarekat Islam (Islamic Union) to acknowledge the growing interest in the movement by Indonesians not associated with business. Its aims were to promote commerce, education, and Islamic principles by encouraging Indonesians to join the village councils being promoted by the government and to enter the administrative service. By 1916, with war waging in Europe, its program was becoming more openly political, calling for the formation of a

Volksraad (People's Council) and the vote for colonial subjects, while still proclaiming loyalty to the Dutch and the principle of nonviolence.

National consciousness received a boost in 1917 from the Bolshevik revolution in Russia, from the entry of the U.S.A. into the war, and from President Wilson's Fourteen Points, which included the principle of self-determination for the minority nationalities of Europe. This concept caught the imagination of Indonesian students. The Russian revolution provided similar inspiration for the small number of Indonesian Communists. The Dutch went so far as to establish in 1918 a Volksraad, which was partly elected and partly nominated but had no real power.

A small Indische Sociaal Democratische Vereeniging (Indies Social-Democratic Association), or ISDV, had been founded by the Dutchman H. J. F. M. Sneevliet in 1914. He and a few other Dutch socialists recruited young Indonesians and prepared them for leadership. Among these were Semaun, Tan Malaka, and Darsono. They infiltrated Sarekat Islam, appealing to those who were frustrated by the lack of progress. Marxism, with its attack on capitalism (represented in Indonesia by Dutch and other foreign business interests) proved attractive and by 1919 Sarekat Islam had two million members and its message had become increasingly nationalist and hostile to the Dutch. This disconcerted the party's more conservative members.

Meanwhile, the Communists formed the Partai Kommunis Indonesia (PKI). For a while the two parties coexisted, the Communists being active in both. However, in 1921 Tjokro Aminoto, leader of Sarekat Islam, was arrested by the Dutch for subversive activities. The Sixth National Congress in 1921 resolved that no member of Sarekat Islam could belong to another political party, forcing the withdrawal of the Communists and returning Sarekat Islam to its Islamic path. Thereafter it lost its domination of the nationalist movement.

Between 1921 and 1926 the PKI dominated the nationalist struggle, focusing on the trade union movement and fomenting economic unrest and strikes, which were rigorously suppressed by the Dutch authorities. Tan Malaka and Semaun were expelled from Indonesia by the Dutch. The remaining leaders, inexperienced and overconfident, believing wrongly that Russia would come to their aid, rose in revolt. The rising was crushed and the PKI banned.

A limited reform of the Volksraad in 1925 did not satisfy nationalist opinion. The PKI failure indicated the futility of open revolt. Students and recent graduates emerged as a new opposition to the Dutch, forming in 1927 what became known in 1928 as the Perserikatan Nasional Indonesia (Indonesian National Party), or PNI. Among its founders and early members were Sukarno, Mohammad Hatta, and Sutan Syahrir. Their objective was independence, their method of achieving it noncooperation with the Dutch. Sukarno was particularly outspoken and especially popular. Together with some other leaders he was arrested in December 1929. In 1930, the party was dissolved by the government.

Of the three splinter parties that then emerged, Partindo (Partai Indonesia—Indonesian Party), founded in April 1931, was the most radical in its policy of noncooperation and appointed Sukarno as its chairman after his release from prison in 1932. The Dutch arrested Sukarno again in 1933, and Mohammad Hatta and Sutan Syahrir the following year. Moderate parties were allowed to function and even nationalists recognized that cooperation with the Dutch without commitment to independence could lead to reform and the creation of a democratically elected parliament.

In May 1939, Gapi (Gabungan Politiek Indonesia—Federation of Indonesian Parties) was formed by the merger of eight political parties. By this time the situation in Europe was coming to a crisis point. In 1940, the Volksraad adopted the Wiwoho Resolution, which sought a conference

on Indonesia's future. The Dutch remained
cautious, but in November offered Indonesians a
greater role in the administration. In June 1941
Queen Wilhelmina, in exile, promised that there
would be a conference to review Indonesia's
postwar position. A step toward this was taken in
September 1941 when a council was established to
consider the creation of a parliament to which the
government in Indonesia would be responsible.
Before more could be done the Japanese invasion
of Southeast Asia had begun.

Japanese Occupation

The Second World War and the Japanese
occupation of the Dutch East Indies weakened the
Netherlands, undermined the prestige of the
Dutch, and revived and armed the independence
movement. The Japanese met little resistance
from the Dutch and a cautious reception from
Indonesians. The Japanese concept of a
Co-Prosperity Sphere appeared to
offer economic promise and the
internment of Dutch officials
opened higher offices to
Indonesians. After attempts to
make Japanese the official

language proved unpopular, the Japanese military
government decided to work with the
nationalists. In March 1943 the Japanese created

Putera (Pusat Tenaga Rakyat— Center of People's Power) with Sukarno as chairman and Hatta as vice-chairman. In September a Central Advisory Board was created, again with Sukarno as chairman, enabling Indonesians to participate in the administration. More important was the creation of Peta (Sukarela Tentera Pembela Tanah Air—Volunteer Army of Defenders of the Homeland), an Indonesian defense force with Indonesian officers.

As the war turned against them, the Japanese attempted to bring the Indonesian nationalists more under their influence, dissolving Putera and creating the Perhimpunan Kebaktian Rakyat (People's Loyalty Association), again with Sukarno as chairman but with the Japanese commander-in-chief in overall control. The Japanese also merged the Islamic parties into one organization, Masyumi (Majelis Syuro Muslimin Indonesia—Consultative Council of Indonesian Muslims), although Muslims could not accept the divinity of the Japanese emperor. The youth organization Angkatan Muda (Young Generation) was also formed in 1944.

The Japanese may have believed they could win the full support of Indonesian nationalists, but the latter were already looking to the future. The creation of these Japanese-sponsored organizations provided platforms for the nationalist cause. Knowing the Japanese aversion to Communism, the national leaders had earlier decided that, while Sukarno and Hatta would collaborate with the Japanese, the PKI leaders Sutan Syahrir, Amir Sjarifuddin, and others would create an underground guerrilla movement to harass them and prepare the way for the arrival of the Allied forces.

Meanwhile, the Japanese, in January 1944, created a Preparatory Committee for Indonesian Independence. On August 8, 1945, the Japanese supreme commander for Southeast Asia announced that independence would be granted on August 24 of that year. It was evident that Japan was near defeat and nationalists urged Sukarno to seize the initiative and announce independence immediately. In any case, an independence granted by Japan would carry little weight. Japan surrendered on August 15. Sukarno declared Indonesia's independence on August 17, and he and Hatta were elected president and vice-president respectively by the Independence Preparatory Committee.

The Pancasila
On June 1, 1945, in a speech to the Independence Preparatory Committee, the future President Sukarno set forth the five fundamental principles, the Pancasila, that would form the basis of an

independent Indonesian state. The purpose of the Five Principles was to provide a broad statement of nationalist aims in a form all Indonesians could accept. Added to the nationalist symbols adopted by the Kongress Rakyat Indonesia (Indonesian People's Congress) in 1939—the national anthem (Indonesia Raya), the red and white national flag displaying the colors of the pre-Islamic Javanese kingdom and empire of Majapahit, and Bahasa Indonesia as the national language—the Pancasila became an important, if vague, expression of nationalist aspirations.

PANCASILA—THE FIVE PRINCIPLES OF THE STATE

1. Belief in the one true God
2. Just and civilized humanity (internationalism)
3. The unity of Indonesia (nationalism)
4. Democracy (representative government)
5. Social justice

The Struggle for Independence

The Dutch attempted to regain control, but were defeated by a combination of Indonesian resistance and international condemnation. British troops arrived in Jakarta on September 29, 1945, their function being to maintain law and order and return authority to the Dutch. By this time Sukarno and his government had been in power for over a month and nationalist support was strong. The Dutch were able to reestablish their authority in the outer islands, but not on Java, where former members of Peta and the anti-Japanese resistance created a national army to resist their return, supported by a mass movement of ardent nationalists known as Pemuda.

Foiled on Java, the Dutch proposed a federal constitution, which would grant the new Republic control of Java, Madura, and Sumatra, to be combined with the rest of the archipelago under Dutch control to form the United States of Indonesia. This, known as the Linggadjati Agreement, was unpopular and, after further violence, Dutch incursions into Republican territory, and a call for a ceasefire by the UN, was replaced by the Renville Agreement negotiated by the U.S.A., Australia, and Belgium, by which plebiscites were to be held to determine which of the main islands wished to be part of the Republic. The Dutch blockaded the Republic while negotiations continued on the implementation of the Agreement, finally launching a further "police action" on Sumatra and Java that resulted in the occupation of major towns and the capture of Sukarno and Hatta. Worldwide criticism of this led to the Hague Round Table Conference in August 1949 and the

eventual transfer of sovereignty of the whole of Indonesia, except Irian Jaya (West New Guinea), to the Republic. On December 27, 1949, Indonesia was proclaimed a sovereign federal republic with Sukarno as president and Hatta as prime minister.

The Sukarno Era
The new Republic was disturbed by regional revolt and political factionalism. In 1950 Sukarno proclaimed the Unitary Republic of Indonesia, replacing the federal system that had proved divisive. The first of the Five Principles, presented by Sukarno as the guiding ideology of the nationalist movement, had been nationalism. With that achieved, the principles have been reordered into their present form. Sukarno furthered the principle of internationalism through Indonesia's membership in the UN and other international bodies and by active

participation in the Non-Aligned Movement, culminating in the Bandung Conference of 1955.

The principle of representative government proved more difficult to achieve. The first general parliamentary elections in 1955 produced no clear majority, the four leading parties gaining between them 78 percent of the votes, but none receiving more than 22.3 percent. The parties, representing the main strands of political opinion, were the Nationalist Party (PNI), the Modernist Muslim Party (Masjumi), the Muslim Theologians' Party (NU), and the Communist Party (PKI). The voting illustrated both regional differences and ideological and social divisions. The balance was such that no coherent policies could be followed and no stable government formed.

Disillusioned with Western-style parliamentary democracy, Sukarno called for a return to the traditional ideals of discussion as practiced at the village level, where the aim was to seek common ground (*musjawarah*) and arrive at a consensus all could accept (*mufakat*). He called for a "Nasakom" government embracing *Nas*ionalism, Religion (*Agama*), and *Kom*unism. Meanwhile, there had been challenges to civilian control by elements in the army.

The failure of this rebellion enhanced Sukarno's position and in 1959 he established a more personal rule in the guise of "Guided Democracy." Increasingly he regarded himself as the personification of the nation, but the economy weakened and his balancing act between a PKI, growing in popularity, and a disillusioned military became increasingly difficult. The invasion and incorporation of Irian Jaya in 1962 was popular, but the campaign of "Confrontation" against the new Federation of Malaysia in 1963–65 proved a failure and tensions grew between the military and the PKI.

On October 1, 1965, a group of radical young army officers kidnapped and murdered six high-ranking generals, who they claimed were plotting against the President. Sukarno failed to support the coup and General Suharto, commanding the elite Army Strategic Reserve, assumed command of the army and suppressed the coup, unleashing bloody reprisals against the PKI and its supporters. Sukarno remained as a figurehead, in March 1966 bestowing wide powers on General Suharto, who was formally installed as president in 1968.

The Suharto Years

Indonesia enjoyed a period of internal stability and economic growth under President Suharto's "New Order." After the attempted coup of 1966 and the declaration of martial law, the PKI and all other Marxist organizations were banned and military personnel were appointed to staff a reorganized civil service. Relations with Russia and China were severed but reestablished with the U.S.A. and other Western powers. Foreign investment was encouraged, inflation was brought under control, and the economy boomed as Indonesia's mineral, oil, and timber resources were developed. Manufacturing expanded as foreign and local investors gained confidence. But this was accompanied by corruption, cronyism, and mismanagement, which would contribute to the regime's decline in popularity.

Though political parties could exist and contest elections, they were closely monitored. Political activity was brought largely under the aegis of Golkar, which was a government-inspired political grouping comprising representatives from military, professional, religious, and ethnic constituencies. The rising middle classes benefited from the economic growth and the development of a consumer society. Widespread poverty persisted, however, as the population grew, despite some success in slowing its spread through family planning. Agricultural developments enabled this population to be fed, but the movement of landless laborers to the cities exceeded the ability of the urban economy to absorb them. The relatively high literacy level produced an urban underclass with relatively ambitious expectations. By the 1990s there was growing dissatisfaction with Suharto's aging leadership and student protests mounted. His government was unable to weather the financial and political crisis of 1997–98 and he resigned in May 1998.

The Suharto regime left a dubious legacy in its 1976 annexation of East Timor. As Portuguese control weakened, a movement known as Fretilin proclaimed independence in November 1975. Fearing the effect this might have on its other outlying territories, such as Aceh and Maluku, Indonesia declared East Timor an integral part of the country, invaded, and in July 1976, after a bloody conflict, incorporated it as the twenty-seventh province. Armed resistance continued and the issue plagued Indonesia thereafter.

Post-Suharto Indonesia
After the departure of Suharto in May 1998, Indonesia reestablished democratic institutions. The new president, Bahruddin Jusof Habibie, moved to settle some of the existing problems. Indonesia recognized East Timor's independence, and Indonesian forces withdrew, a move approved by world opinion, but leaving Timor severely

crippled and destitute. The separatist movement in Aceh, however, remained intractable. Other pressures that had simmered beneath the surface during the later Suharto years became more evident, but not necessarily more dangerous to the integrity of the state. These included the recurrent tension between fundamentalist Islam and secularism, and between Java, with the majority of the population, and the outer provinces, with most of the natural resources.

Habibie was replaced as president in October 2000 by Abdurrahman Wahid, who in turn was defeated in the elections of July 2001 by Megawati Sukarnoputri, the daughter of the late President Sukarno. Coming in on a wave of enthusiastic support based upon the magic of her name, her government produced political stability but had only limited success with the economy. The Bali bombing of October 21, 2002, undermined confidence, seriously weakening the troubled tourist industry and the economy in general.

The fear of further terrorism, the failure to end the separatist threat in Aceh, and continued problems with the economy contributed to the defeat of Megawati and the election of President Susilo Bambang Yudoyono in October 2004. In December of that year, the Asian tsunami wrought havoc on the coast of Aceh, striking a further blow at tourism in the region.

Despite this catalogue of woe, Indonesia is not on the brink of collapse. It has coped with the terrorist threat and with the tsunami disaster. It has a stable system of government, its economy is developing, and its international and regional position is respected. It is a vast country: many regions have been untouched by unrest, while in others the troubles have passed. Its economic potential continues to attract investment, its scenic and cultural attractions are remarkable, and the people are as welcoming as ever.

THE PEOPLES OF INDONESIA

There are more than three hundred ethnic groups in Indonesia, each with its own culture. Modernization, education, and migration out of their home areas is to some extent blurring the distinctions between them, but most of those you will meet in Jakarta and other cities retain their links with their villages and are proud of their origins. There are some distinctive groups about whom you should have some knowledge.

Sumatra

The **Acenese** of northern Sumatra are a product of centuries of intermarriage with those who traveled the trade route between Arabia, India, and China, including Arabs, Chinese, Indians,

Javanese, and other Indonesian and Malay groups and slaves from the island of Nias. The people are slim and almost Caucasian in appearance. Mainly agriculturalists, they are also recognized as fine metalworkers, weavers, potters, and boat builders. Islam was introduced in the thirteenth century, but more ancient beliefs in magic and evil spirits coexist with it, particularly with regard to illness, the interpretation of dreams, and agriculture. Brought late under Dutch rule, the Acenese remain a fiercely independent people. Personal names tend to sound Arabic.

The **Batak** inhabit the interior of north-central Sumatra around Lake Toba. Largely isolated until the mid-nineteenth century, they are regarded by anthropologists as representative of the ancient proto-Malay cultures of the archipelago. The Batak trace their ancestry back to a hero called Si Radja Batak, born of supernatural parentage on a holy rock near Lake Toba. With a reputation for having practiced ritual cannibalism, they came under the influence of the Rheinische Mission and those around Lake Toba are mainly Christian. The Batak are renowned for their distinctive houses, whose roofs feature large gable ends and carved buffalo horns. They have complicated marriage traditions, court each other with poetry contests, and have produced many popular singers and entertainers. Common names include Sinaga, Simatupang, Silitonga, Pangabean, Hutapea, Simanjuntak, Hutasoit, Sembiring, Lubis, Nasution, and Tobang.

The **Minangkabau** live in west-central Sumatra. Their provincial capital is Padang and, like the Batak, their houses are distinctive, having a large, sweeping, curved roof. Unusually, they have accommodated Islam with a matrilineal social system: women have high status, control the household, and inheritance is through the female line. The Minangkabau traveled widely as traders, and trade as merchants and shopkeepers. Many also settled on the Malayan peninsula in what is now the Malaysian state of Selangor. Like the Batak, they believe in a large number of spirits. Minangkabau names often sound Islamic and often include the letter "z" as in Rizal or Faizal.

Java

The **Javanese** are the most numerous group on Java and in Indonesia as a whole. The name Java comes from the Sanskrit *yawa*, meaning barley. The traditional villages are small, perhaps containing up to three thousand people,

the buildings clustered in groves of trees surrounded by fields. Rice is the main crop, grown in small, fragmented landholdings. The majority of peasants are landless agricultural laborers. In many areas cash crops are grown on larger holdings. The written form of the Javanese language dates from the eleventh century and derives from Sanskrit used in the Hindu courts. It is very sophisticated, with nine levels reflecting rank, status, age, and degree of acquaintance between speakers, reflecting its origin in a highly stratified society. Even family names reflect status (elder, younger) rather than sex (sister, brother).

The Javanese developed sophisticated kingdoms, their culture still visible in the courts of Yogyakarta and Surakarta. The *wayang kulit* (shadow play) continues a tradition derived from India and portrays the characters of the Hindu classics. Performances are accompanied by a *gamelan* orchestra comprising a range of bronze gongs and other percussive instruments.

Javanese often have only one name. Upper-class Javanese will choose a family name. Common family names often end in "o," as in Sukarno, Suharto, Sartono, Hadikusoimo.

The **Sundanese** are from the Priangan Highlands of West Java. Their culture is similar to that of the Javanese, but with subtle differences. Thus, instead of the *wayang kulit* using leather puppets, the Sundanese *wayang golek* has wooden puppets. Their music is associated with the flute (*suling*) rather than the *gamelan.*

Also in West Java, the **Badui** are a small isolated community who support themselves by slash-and-burn agriculture and hunting. They are also known for picking and collecting the much prized durian fruit. The families of the three inner villages claim descent from the gods and avoid outside contact. The outer villages are more accessible, but little interested in the outside world. They call themselves either Orang Kanekes, after their sacred territory, or Orang Parahiang, after a mythological territory inhabited by spirits. It is thought that they may have fled from the ancient kingdom of Pajajaran when it was attacked in 1579 by the Muslim Bantamese. They have an elaborate mythology; many of their deities bear Hindu names. They consider writing to have magic power and use inscribed sticks in their ceremonies: the writings are thought to be the remnants of a largely forgotten indigenous script. The Badui are an example of how, even on a crowded island like Java, small, little-known populations survive.

Bali

The **Balinese** are a blend of Mongoloid peoples with linguistic links to the Sasaks of Lombok and to Java. They and their culture are widely known outside Indonesia and the island has long attracted artists and travelers. Popular tourism has been encouraged since the 1950s. Over the centuries Hinduism on the island has taken on a Balinese form and is expressed through communal ritual and drama with emphasis on myth and legend. These forms of storytelling were easily transformed into performances for tourists, just as the traditional arts and crafts have been adapted for the tourist market. In the countryside, the terraced rice fields covering the slopes of the hills are fed by sophisticated irrigation systems. Villages consist of walled compounds housing the family homes, which comprise a series of rooms, courtyards, and shrines. The Balinese believe in spirits, which have to be placated. They perform elaborate cremation ceremonies whereby the soul is released after death. Families trace their descent from a deity or a location and status is reflected in their names.

Sulawesi

The **Toraja** of south-central Sulawesi are a highland people farming the fertile inland valleys. Related to the Bugis, they arrived from the sea many generations ago and moved inland up the Sa'adan River. Their houses, raised on stilts, have roofs that rise at both ends like the bow and stern of a boat. Buffalo (and their horns) are status symbols. They practice an elaborate form of cliff burial: effigies of the dead are left in open galleries in the cliff face. In recent years, with improved access to the area, these burials have become a tourist attraction.

The **Bugis** of south Sulawesi, related to the Toraja, were renowned seafarers and boatbuilders, often referred to as "Sea Gypsies," because in foreign ports many lived with their families on their boats. Their main port was Makassar, which accepted Islam in the seventeenth century and was the preeminent power in the region until its conquest by the Dutch. The Bugis combined trading with piracy, but also settled on the coasts and estuaries of Sulawesi and Kalimantan and on offshore islands. Many still trade between the islands in their distinctive and colorful sailed craft, these days often with an auxiliary engine. The Bugis also produce high-quality silk, much sought after in the region. They have a reputation for being proud, aggressive, and outspoken (partly a product of their past reputation), and their dynamism serves them well in the modern world.

The **Minahasa** live in the northern part of Sulawesi, where Manado is the main city. The majority are agriculturalists. Their languages indicate past links with the Philippines, but intermarriage with Chinese and Europeans has produced a largely Eurasian population. Mostly Christianized, they have lost many of their traditional customs and crafts other than folk dancing. The agricultural cycle is celebrated with ceremony, singing, dancing, drinking, and feasting at times of planting and harvest. Westerners feel comfortable in their company and the region has become popular with vacationers.

Kalimantan (Borneo)

Dayak is the name generally given to any of the many groups of non-Muslim indigenous people, whose Mongoloid ancestors arrived many millennia ago. Generally light skinned, they resemble the Chinese, but have evolved in isolation. They now live along the rivers of Kalimantan in semipermanent settlements, traditionally longhouses, practicing shifting cultivation, fishing, gathering jungle produce, and hunting, often still with spear and blowpipe. Dayaks believe in ancestral spirits and in spirits resident in natural objects. Headhunting was once endemic and longhouses, most with elaborately carved doorposts and pillars, retain collections of skulls obtained in the past. Women are famed for their weaving, beadwork, and basketry, using highly intricate anthropomorphic and stylized designs depicting animals, birds, and other creatures. Women have high status and may be shamans with powers of healing. Despite the old reputation for taking heads, Dayaks are hospitable to guests. Government policy is encouraging single-house settlement and the planting of cash crops. Dayak men have always made journeys to trade and work, and many are settling on the fringes of towns and cities or near timber camps.

The **overseas Chinese** are the most important alien group in Indonesia. The largest populations are in Java, eastern Sumatra, and western Kalimantan, but they are to be found everywhere.

Chinese have been living in Indonesia for centuries, particularly in the ports trading with China. Many who arrived returned eventually to their homeland, as was usually their intention, but a large number did not do so, and became absorbed into the population.

The big influx of Chinese occurred in the nineteenth century, when the Dutch colonial government recruited labor for plantations and mines. In this they were following in the steps of some local rulers who had recruited Chinese for similar purposes. The rulers of Sambas, in west Kalimantan, for example, had encouraged Chinese *kongsis* (Cantonese *Kung Sz*, a business partnership) to operate the gold mines, taxing them for the privilege. Chinese merchants, traders, and shopkeepers were involved in the business of recruiting labor and supplying its needs. They opened small shops and went into trade. It was competition from Chinese batik traders that prompted the creation of the Islamic traders' movement (see page 23). Chinese who made good were encouraged by the Dutch to move into commercial and financial enterprises and many were recruited into foreign firms. In the early twentieth century, Chinese women were allowed to emigrate to Indonesia, thus laying the foundation for more permanent settlement. The Chinese became key players in the economy, a position resented by many indigenous Indonesians, leading on occasion to anti-Chinese demonstrations and riots. Their pivotal role has come to be accepted, however.

For census purposes, the Chinese are classified in two groups: the *penerakan* Chinese, who tend to be assimilated and to identify themselves as Indonesians whose future lies in Indonesia, and the *totok* Chinese, who are less integrated and more China-oriented. It is sometimes difficult for an outsider to recognize a *penerakan* Chinese because many have taken Indonesian names.

THE ECONOMY

Although Indonesia weathered the Asian financial crisis, its economy still faces problems inherited from the past. These include an inadequate infrastructure, unequal resource distribution among the regions, corruption, a weak banking sector, and high unemployment. The oil industry has suffered from lack of investment and production has been declining; the country became a net importer of oil in 2004. Almost half of the labor force is engaged in agriculture, about 12 percent in industry, and 42 percent in services. Much depends on attracting investors and on the growth of the global economy. Indonesia suffered from the Indian Ocean tsunami in December 2004, and tourism, an important source of revenue, has been affected by terrorist incidents in 2005 and by concern about avian influenza.

GOVERNMENT

Indonesia is a republic with a president who is both head of state and head of government. The cabinet is appointed by the president. The president and vice-president are elected by universal suffrage to serve five-year terms. The age of voting is seventeen.

There are three legislative bodies. The House of Representatives (Dewan Perwakilan Rakyat), or DPR, has 550 members serving five-year terms. The House of Regional Representation (Dewan Perwakilan Daerah), or DPD, discusses legislation affecting the regions. The People's Consultative Assembly (Mejelis Permusyawaratan Rakyat), or MPR, consisting of popularly elected members in the DPR and DPD, has the role of inaugurating and impeaching a president and in amending the constitution. It does not formulate national policy. There are a number of political parties and the government is a coalition.

The judiciary is headed by the Supreme Court (Mahkamah Agung), whose members are appointed by the president from a list of candidates approved by the legislature. The independence of the judiciary has been enhanced since 2004, when the Supreme Court assumed administrative and financial responsibility for the lower court system from the Ministry of Justice.

The legal system is based on Roman-Dutch law, considerably modified by indigenous legal concepts. *Shariah* law is not applied.

chapter two

VALUES & ATTITUDES

Indonesia is a nation comprising a great variety of peoples and cultures, all of which are being affected by Western, "modern" values and attitudes purveyed through the media, films, satellite television, the Internet, education, commerce, and tourism. Nevertheless, the basic family and social values remain and form a basis for interpersonal relations and public behavior. Despite their diversity, similar values underpin all Indonesian societies and the comments below apply to all.

THE FAMILY

The family is Indonesia's central institution. It defines one's position in life and provides security, status, and identity. The extended family is alive and well in Indonesia, and family relationships are clearly defined. The recognized head of the family is the eldest male, affectionately known as *bapak,* and members are ranked by age rather then sex, down to the newly born. Infants remain in close contact with their mothers and are carried everywhere. Fathers are affectionate to their children, who are taught to respect and honor them, though the relationship becomes more distant as they grow up. Where there are a large number of children, the elder siblings may spend some time away living with other relatives. An older relative may take a mentoring role as "uncle" or "aunt," but the parents retain the position of highest honor.

The communal aspects of living in an extended family provide security but also responsibilities. In particular, children are expected to care for their parents throughout their life and, if living away, to contribute to their welfare. Elder children look after their younger siblings and, when working, are expected to contribute toward their education. To a certain extent the individual is restricted by these duties; on the other hand, the family provides refuge and safety.

Linked to these obligations is the concept of communal property. Many family members may live in the same house, their ages spanning the generations. Members of the family may come and go. Wealth and possessions are shared, and there is little regard for what the Westerner regards as personal or private property. The strong sense of family and community means that individual interests are subordinated to the collective, producing a higher degree of conformity than in Western societies.

The Hawaiian Shirt

A European married to an Indonesian had a favorite, colorful Hawaiian shirt. He soon noticed that his wife's brother, who was staying with them, was wearing it. When asked to return it, the young man shrugged and did so, but at every opportunity he "borrowed" it again. To him it was not impolite to enter his brother-in-law's room and take the shirt to wear. He did not intend to keep it, although if it had been given to him he would have accepted it gladly. Equally, however, he did not object when his brother-in-law casually "borrowed" items from him without asking, at first to make a point, later because he came to accept the situation.

SOCIAL BEHAVIOR

Outside the family a similar respect for age and hierarchy prevails. Indonesians will attempt to establish your place in the order of things. You will be questioned politely about your own family, whether you are married and have children, your occupation, and your general background. This may appear inquisitive, but is not meant as an intrusion. Indonesians regard it as good manners and will be genuinely interested in the details you disclose. Perhaps more importantly, they will be able to treat you with what is in their terms proper respect. In their eyes, it would be discourteous to you and shameful to them if they did not properly address you and treat you as your social position warranted.

Once your status has been established you may have bestowed upon you a title relating to your age or status or, if you become friendly with the family, a kinship term. You may in this case also be drawn into some of the obligations of family and kinship. Indonesian society is made up of a web of such interactions, hierarchies, and obligations, and there is a higher degree of conformity than in Western societies. These attitudes affect social behavior in both public and private life. The visitor needs to be aware of what constitutes good behavior in order to avoid unintentionally giving offense.

Getting To Know You

If asked questions about your personal life, be prepared to respond politely and to ask similar questions. It is courteous to do so, and those you ask will feel that you wish to know and understand their status in their society in order to define their status within your life. It also provides a ready topic of conversation when you first meet people.

The Importance of Harmony

Indonesians place great value upon social harmony, and behaving according to custom maintains harmony. Indonesians dislike a "scene." The concept of "face" is important and no one should be treated with less than respect in public. Bluntness is rude, loudness is vulgar, and aggressiveness is bad manners.

In practical terms, whether it be planning a joint activity or reaching a business decision, discussions and making decisions can take more time than many Westerners expect. Indonesians express differences of opinion in a manner that you might find irritating and devious. For example, Indonesians are reluctant to say "no." There are politer ways to express a negative or to indicate that something has not been done. Indonesians are sensitive to nuances of speech and expression and will understand what to you may remain vague and opaque. It follows that if you infer correctly that something has gone wrong or a task has not been completed on time you should yourself be careful how you respond. In general, in any situation, the aim is to arrive at a consensus that satisfies "face" on all sides.

The process may, however, produce delays in and adjustments to the execution of decisions. While this may be frustrating, losing your temper would only cause embarrassment, be unproductive, and lower the respect in which you are held. The best recourse is to retain a sense of humor, accept the elasticity of time, and be firm in maintaining your own position with courtesy, while seeking a compromise that involves no loss of face for either party. Not liking to say "no," themselves, Indonesians dislike blunt rejection of their own views and proposals. They will, though, eventually accept a compromise.

SOCIAL HARMONY: KEY CONCEPTS

Gotong royong working together, mutual cooperation

Mesyuarat discussion, mutual exchange of views with respect for individual views and avoidance of loss of face

Muafakat consensus, mutual agreement

FLEXIBLE TIME

In Indonesia, time is elastic. People operate to a different sense of time. Punctuality is not ingrained. Relationships are more important, so a friend never needs to make an appointment, nor is it polite to bring a meeting to an end hastily. Government offices apparently have set hours, but the individuals you wish to see may keep to more flexible times. Things get done, but not necessarily to a timetable. If a meeting has been arranged, or if you have reason to deal with a government department, take a book and go with the flow.

British Time?
A friend from England was visiting Jakarta and wanted the use of a car, with a driver. At his hotel he ordered the car for 8:30 the next morning. "Is that Indonesian or British time, Sir?" he was asked. He was taken aback until he realized that the driver was trying to confirm whether he had to present himself at that hour precisely or whether the exact time was of little importance.

ATTITUDES TO FOREIGNERS
Courtesy to strangers is normal. Indonesians will regard you as a guest in their country and if you live and work there you will soon have Indonesian friends. In tourist areas courtesy may be tinged with commercial expectations and touts, or scalpers, may be a problem but, generally, foreigners are treated as welcome guests. Away from areas where foreigners congregate you may be an object of curiosity, but Indonesia has for centuries been a center of trade where foreigners have been well received. Whatever tensions may

arise within Indonesia between peoples and regions are not directed at foreigners. Terrorist incidents are as abnormal in Indonesia as they are in London and horrify the average Indonesian.

MAKING THE RIGHT IMPRESSION

Relations with your Indonesian hosts can be smoothed if you understand and respect their sensibilities. In the tourist resorts certain behavior is tolerated, though not admired, but people who offend local susceptibilities will receive less respect. Whether you are a tourist or are working in the country, you will improve your standing if you conform to local norms of behavior.

Dress

In most of Indonesia, what to wear is largely determined by the Muslim code of dress, which is that both men and women should dress modestly. In general terms this means that most of the body should be covered. Clothing should not be tight fitting or revealing. In practical terms, shorts may be worn by children, bathers, and for sport, but not in the street. In private you can wear what you like and in tourist areas and beach resorts scanty clothing is accepted. When visiting conservative Muslim areas it is only polite to dress modestly.

General dress for men is a loose cotton shirt worn with light trousers and comfortable shoes or sandals. Women should wear a cotton blouse with long or three-quarter-length sleeves and a skirt reaching below the knees, or a dress providing similar covering, and light, comfortable shoes or sandals. A bra should be worn at all times.

When meeting Indonesians in some official or formal capacity or attending a business meeting, men should wear a lightweight suit or a long-sleeved shirt and tie. Women should wear a below-knee-length skirt and smart long-sleeved blouse, or a long-sleeved dress, but not pants.

For formal social occasions such as weddings and receptions, dress is usually indicated on the invitation. Men may be permitted to wear a long-sleeved batik shirt. These are of cotton and are colorfully patterned, smart, and cool.

If visiting a mosque, women should cover their heads and legs. Men should not wear shorts. If improperly dressed, you may be required to wear a voluminous gown or not be allowed in at all. In Bali you will need to tie a scarf around your waist in order to enter a temple; many provide these.

In some areas and in some circumstances codes do differ, but first impressions are important and it is better to err on the side of caution. Dress conservatively until you can gauge the attitude of your Indonesian hosts and companions.

CAMERAS

The camera-laden tourist has become a comic
cliché, but all of us become unthinking voyeurs
through the viewfinder. Indonesia, particularly
Bali, offers a wealth of photo opportunities, but
remember that the ceremonies and rites you
come across are not staged for your benefit.
Unless you are an invited guest, keep a discreet
distance. There is always a balance to be struck.
In tourist areas there are staged performances,
which you may photograph and film at will.

Always ask permission before taking a
photograph of a person, unless your telephoto
lens is good enough to do so without intrusion.
Most Indonesians cannot afford cameras and in
some areas will happily be photographed.
Unfortunately, they may take this as a very
serious and solemn occasion. Usually a quick
second shot will catch them relaxed and smiling.
If people have allowed you to photograph them,
take their names and addresses, if possible, so
that a copy may be sent—and do so if at all
possible.

Among Indonesian friends the situation is
obviously different, but remember that you
remain a guest. The arrival of the cheap digital
camera has made photography available to an
increasing number of younger Indonesians, so in
some quarters attitudes are relaxed.

chapter three

RELIGION & FESTIVALS

RELIGION

Religion is important in everyday life. Islam is the religion of 80 percent of the population, making Indonesia the largest Muslim country in the world, but there are substantial Buddhist, Hindu, Christian, and animist populations. The island of Bali is predominantly Hindu, and there are Christian communities in Sulawesi, Maluku, and Kalimantan. Belief in God is the first tenet of the Pancasila, the Five Principles that define the state. The language of the Pancasila and of the state motto, *Bhinneka Tunggal Ika* ("They are many: They are one;" also translated as "Unity in Diversity"), is Sanskrit, the language of Hindu scripture. Islam in Indonesia rests on Hindu and animist foundations, which long predate its arrival and pervade Indonesian culture, which is imbued with the themes, stories, and characters of the great Hindu epics, the *Ramayana* and the *Mahabharata.*

Buddhism was also established, exemplified in the great ninth-century monument of Borobudur in central Java, but is now practiced largely by urban Indonesians of Chinese descent. Islam established itself in the fifteenth century, firstly in Aceh and then on Java, where it triumphed in the sixteenth century. In that century, too, Christianity arrived in its Catholic manifestation with the Portuguese. It was introduced in its Protestant form with the Dutch in the seventeenth century. Christianity retains strongholds in the outer islands, such as Ambon, North Sulawesi, and Kalimantan, and has many adherents throughout the archipelago. Animism remains prevalent in Kalimantan and Irian Jaya, although under pressure from Islam and Christianity, and animist beliefs continue to permeate popular culture, even on Java.

Religion infiltrates the lives of Indonesians to an extent no longer true in much of the West. Do not be afraid to ask people their religion, for it is a useful guide to how to act in their presence. It would be improper to offer alcohol to a Muslim and offensive to offer pork. It would be equally offensive to offer beef to a Hindu. Also important to a Muslim is the method of slaughter. Any meat they eat should have been slaughtered according to Muslim law and thus rendered *halal*. On their part, Indonesians will assume that a Westerner is Christian. They are likely to be distressed if you claim that you have no religion.

Islam

There is no state religion in Indonesia, but Islam is the religion of most Indonesians, and visitors should be aware of its main tenets and practices in order not to offend unintentionally. Carried to Indonesia by traders and individuals, Islam gained acceptance through accommodation and absorption rather than by conquest. Toleration of other religions is embodied in the Pancasila. There is a small minority of Muslims who would welcome a stricter observance of Islam, including the introduction of *shariah* law, but the moderate majority are content with current practices.

The five principles of Islam that all adherents should observe are the confession of faith, the performance of the ritual prayer five times a day, the payment of the religious tax, observing the fast of Ramadan, and performing the pilgrimage (*haj*) to Mecca.

Muslims are expected to pray five times a day—at sunrise, just after the sun has reached its zenith, just before sunset, soon after sunset, and again at night. Not all individuals perform all these prayers, but attendance at the mosques on Fridays is high. If near a mosque, you will become accustomed to the call to prayer, traditionally called from the minaret by the iman, but these days often recorded and amplified. A non-Muslim should avoid visiting a mosque at these times.

Before praying, purification rites are performed, in the following order: washing the hands with water three times from the wrist down; gargling and spitting to clean the mouth; washing the face; washing both arms from wrist to elbow; moistening part of the head, combing the hair with water; and washing both feet up to the ankles. Mosques, therefore, have washing areas attached. Men wear a plain shirt and a sarong to the mosque and may also carry their prayer mat (*sedajah*). Women wear a long garment known as the *mukena*, though it is usual for women to pray at home. The Friday midday prayer is the best attended and government offices close for that period. Given the pressures of normal life, most other prayers are performed away from the mosque, at home or at the place of work. Most commercial and office buildings have a *musholla*, a room set aside for prayer. If invited to or staying in a Muslim household, be careful not to intrude on any person performing prayers.

Visiting a Mosque
Visitors are generally welcome, but remember that it is a holy place and act accordingly. It is polite to ask permission of any person who may be around. Men should wear long trousers and

women a garment with long sleeves and a long skirt rather than pants. If inappropriately dressed, both men and women may be offered a gown to cover the offending garments. Remove shoes before entering the mosque and behave quietly and respectfully when inside. Walk behind any persons who may be praying, ask permission before taking photographs, and be careful not to touch anything, especially the Holy Koran. You may find that a custodian accompanies you.

Hinduism

Hinduism survives on the island of Bali, but elsewhere, particularly on Java, the art, music, and culture of Indonesia are profoundly affected by the great Hindu epics, the *Ramayana* and the *Mahabharata*. Indonesian Muslims and Christians know these stories, attend performances of them, and may dance and act in them. Throughout the archipelago, beliefs in more ancient deities and spirits persist and influence the way people behave. Do not be surprised if someone you have learned is a Christian or a Muslim offers gifts to the spirits before embarking on some enterprise. It is akin to superstitious practices that persist in the West, often spoken of in jest, but still in the folk memory—such as touching wood for luck.

Hedging Your Bets

My wife and I were traveling to Bandung from Jakarta in a minibus. We had negotiated the crowded streets of the city and were leaving them behind, with the main road clearly before us. Suddenly, the driver pulled to the side and leapt out to place an offering at a roadside shrine, which looked more Hindu than Muslim. "For a safe journey," he remarked as we swung out again into the stream of chaotic traffic. One could appreciate the desire to cover all the bases.

Semangat and Spirits

Indonesians believe all living things are endowed with a life force known as *semangat*. Indeed it may also be embodied in sacred objects, a weapon such as a *kris* (dagger), or in places of ritual or sacred significance. In persons it is concentrated in the head and its hair, hence the prohibition on touching them. Many marriage rites include the exchange of locks of hair or plaiting together the hair of the bride and groom. The first cutting of an infant's hair is often solemnized by a *selamatan,* or celebration. Hair and nail clippings are important ingredients in love potions and spells designed to increase ardor or to work harm, and are carefully disposed of in order to prevent them falling into the hands of someone who may use them for this purpose.

Blood is also imbued with *semangat* and plays a role in many rituals. The ritual battles performed on Flores and Sumba, animal sacrifice, and in some regions the anointing with blood of the pillars of newly constructed houses are all indicative of beliefs involving in certain places human as well as animal sacrifice. The tradition that a *kris* once drawn must taste blood, and the practice in old Makassar that the royal regalia should be washed in blood, both relate to the belief in blood as a bearer of *semangat.*

More benign are the spirits of plants, most importantly that of rice. Variations of a pre-Islamic legend associate the rice spirit with a beautiful woman who preferred death to dishonor and from whose remains the rice plant (and in some versions other food plants) grew. On Bali, she is worshiped as Dewi Sri and temples are dedicated to her. As a consequence, the rice cycle throughout Indonesia is also a religious observance and ritual directs the pattern of the year's farming activity. This respect for the spirits of nature extends to other crops and to hunting and gathering. Rituals and prayers are performed to increase fertility, to ensure good yields, and to appease the spirits, which inhabit all living things.

Natural features like mountains or lakes may also acquire *semangat*. Places that are in some way distinctive in form or are associated with holy or great men or with mythical beings; objects that are distinctive, malformed, or out of the ordinary; old artifacts, heirlooms, weapons, or treasures: all may embody a soul or spiritual essence that may have to be revered or appeased.

Spirits may be "good" or "bad." Indonesian folklore is haunted by *hantu-hantu* or ghosts. These are the spirits of those who have suffered a violent death. A frequent subject of popular Indonesian horror films is the *pontianak*, the spirit of a woman who has died in childbirth. Evil spirits like these must be placated or exorcized by shamans, who also treat afflictions and ailments of various kinds suffered by people, livestock, and crops. The biggest exorcism of all is held on Bali the day before the Balinese New Year, when evil spirits are driven away with great noise.

FESTIVALS
Islamic Festivals

Islamic festivals are recognized by national public holidays and are based on the Muslim calendar, which moves back eleven days each year according to the Western calendar.

ISLAMIC FESTIVALS
Muharan Muslim New Year
Maulud Nabi Muhammad Birthday of the Prophet Muhammad
Ascension Day of Muhammad
Idul Fitri The end of Ramadan, the fasting month
Idul Adha (Day of Sacrifice) Commemorating Abraham's willingness to sacrifice his son, Ishmael (Ismail)

During Ramadan, the ninth month of the Muslim year, believers fast from dawn to dusk. You should not eat, drink, or smoke in public or in the presence of Muslims at this time, or offer food or drink to Muslims. Muslim friends and colleagues will break their fast at sunset and restaurants and food stalls, many of which are closed during the day, will be open in the evening. The end of Ramadan is a time of feasting and visiting. Maintaining the fast is no light achievement in a hot, humid, enervating climate. Sleep is also reduced by the need to rise early to prepare food and eat. While modern offices will have air-conditioning, it does not alleviate hunger and thirst. During the fast, Muslim employees and colleagues should be treated with consideration. Some may show signs of stress before Ramadan is over. This does not excuse them from performing their normal tasks and duties, but there should be an element of flexibility where this is possible. Individual exceptions exist and not every Muslim will observe the fast to the letter. As a non-Muslim and a guest in the country, however, you should assume that all do until convinced otherwise.

Hindu Festivals
Bali is the center for Hinduism in Indonesia and observes the Hindu festivals. There is always a celebration somewhere in Bali. Each of the island's twenty thousand temples marks an anniversary based on a calendar of 210 days.

BALI: ISLAND-WIDE CELEBRATIONS
Galungan
A ten-day celebration of the triumph of good over evil, the last day of which, known as Kuningan, is the most important. Occurs at intervals of 210 days.

Nyepi, the Balinese New Year
Held March/April. On New Year's Eve evil spirits are driven out with fireworks and the beating of drums. On the day itself, everyone stays quietly indoors to convince the evil spirits that the island is uninhabited; visitors are expected to do the same.

Balinese ceremonies from weddings to funerals are communal celebrations. No one will object to your discreet presence, but do not intrude unless invited to participate.

If you are in a tourist area, regular performances of dance and drama provide some insight into Balinese culture, though without the spontaneity and involvement of the real thing.

Other islands have celebrations and festivals, which you may ask about when in Indonesia at the time you intend to travel.

CHRISTIAN FESTIVALS

March/April	Good Friday and Easter Sunday
May/June	Ascension Day
December 25	Christmas Day

NATIONAL AND OTHER CELEBRATIONS

In addition to the Muslim holy days, national public holidays include:

January 1 Tahun Baru (New Year's Day)

January/February Imlek (Chinese New Year. Most Chinese businesses close for two or more days.)

March Waisak Day (birth, death, and enlightenment of Buddha)

April 21 Kartini Day (Women's Day, named after the writer)

August 17 Independence Day

October Armed Forces Day

RITES OF PASSAGE

All societies celebrate in some form the rites of passage associated with birth, puberty, marriage, and death. In Indonesia these are communal events in which the whole community (if in a village), or the extended family, friends, neighbors, and business and work associates (if in a town or city) will be involved.

They are also matters of spiritual significance. Underlying all belief systems in Indonesia is respect for the spirits residing in holy places, in natural objects, and in living things. Thus many actions a Westerner considers routine and secular have a spiritual significance in Indonesia. A Muslim slaughtering an animal will utter a prayer; a farmer harvesting rice will pray or make offerings to the rice spirit; a taxi driver proceeding on a journey may make an offering at a shrine; a businessman before making a decision may seek guidance from a medium. How much more important, therefore, are those events that mark out the life of the individual and of the community. The observance of such events is defined by *adat* or custom, the traditional way.

Selamatan

A celebration is always accompanied by a feast, which brings members of a community together. The Indonesian word for such a celebration is *selamatan* (safeguarding), which has overtones of prosperity and happiness. A *selamatan* is held to mark a birth, circumcision, marriage, death, anniversary, the commencement of a new project, or to bring prosperity and good fortune. The basic traditional form on Java is the eating of an inverted cone of colored rice and ritually slaughtered meats, the recitation of Islamic prayers, and the burning of incense. The host makes formal requests and announcements in keeping with the occasion.

MUSLIM CEREMONIES
Bersanding
The *selamatan* you are most likely to be invited to as a friend, colleague, or neighbor will be a

bersanding, equivalent to a Western wedding reception, held after vows have been exchanged. As in all cultures, a wedding is a joyous occasion and one requiring a public acknowledgment of the union not only of the couple, but of their families. If the family is "modern," it may be held at a restaurant or hotel, but usually it is at the bride's home, to which the bridegroom is escorted in procession by his retinue. As part of the ceremony the couple receive the blessings of those invited. As a guest you can send a small gift of money in a wedding card to the bride's home or pass it discreetly to a member of the bride's family as they stand in line to greet the visitors.

The bride and groom will normally be attired in rich costumes and enthroned to receive the blessings of the guests. They are expected to remain still and unresponsive: at village weddings attempts may be made to distract them and an element of bawdiness creeps in. As an honored guest, you may be asked to perform the ritual of blessing. You will be shown what to do and will have opportunity to observe others. At the end of the ceremony the bride and groom may circulate among the guests, who have been seated at tables for the wedding feast. At a traditional wedding,

men and women will be seated separately; you will be conducted to your seat and food brought to you. At modern weddings, seating may be mixed and food served buffet style.

A Rustic Wedding

We were invited to a village wedding. To get there we had to walk along a track from a dirt road. The village was small and the *bersanding* was held on cleared ground among the few houses. The bride and groom sat in their finery in a colorfully decorated arbor. As we approached, we noticed that a pair of trousers hung from the bride's bedroom window, suggesting to the young man as his entourage arrived that a rival had beaten him to it. During the course of the *bersanding* the village practical joker climbed one of the young banana palms on the edge of the clearing and began suggestively peeling the fronds back. The young couple studiously ignored the scene despite the laughter and ribald comments.

Birth

Ceremonies associated with the birth of a baby are traditionally communal. Not surprisingly these are linked with prayers that the baby be healthy and strong.

Practices differ between the different ethnic and religious groups and persist in their most traditional form in the villages. Some ceremonies take place seven days after the birth, when the mother takes the baby into the village for the first time. These may simply involve the distribution of a specially prepared rice cake, or a more elaborate ceremony involving ritual bathing and a procession. In Christian areas food is provided after baptism. Whatever the ceremonial, the child is welcomed into the community.

Two ceremonies practiced widely throughout Indonesia are deeply rooted in past animist and Hindu rituals. One, known as *tujuh bulan,* is a form of ritual bathing for the expectant mother, usually at the seventh month of pregnancy; although in Bali it is the third month. The communal nature of the prayers and ritual provide emotional support to the mother. The rituals vary, but involve scented water, flowers, fruit, cloth, and food. Some groups, such as the Toba Batak, may have a *selamatan* without the ritual bathing.

The second traditional ceremony is *turun tanah,* which introduces the child to the earth and welcomes it into the family and the community. In Bali it is held after 210 days, the Balinese year; in other communities earlier, but not before a month or forty days has passed since the birth.

During that month most mothers rest, although "modern" mothers begin to socialize earlier. During the *selamatan*, the baby's hair is cut, gifts are bestowed, and attempts made to divine his or her future. Batik cloth is an acceptable gift. Cloth presented at these ceremonies is often kept for the life of the individual.

Circumcision (*sunatan*)

While not compulsory, it is customary for Muslim boys to undergo circumcision at the age of eleven or twelve. Once a public event marking the passage to manhood, it is commonly now simply a medical procedure. Traditionally it was followed by a procession through the village, which is still the case in parts of Java. Usually a *selamatan* will be held for family and friends. Should you be invited, money is an appropriate gift for the boy.

Death

Muslims generally bury their dead within twenty-four hours. Relatives, friends, and neighbors are expected to attend the funeral and the preceding ceremonies; there will be much activity as they arrive and start helping with the preparations. The body is prepared for burial by members of the family, the head facing Mecca, and passages from the Koran are read over it. The local iman ritually cleanses the body with pure perfumed water and it is wrapped in three layers of seamless cloth. Before the face is covered, the family and friends view the deceased for a final farewell and say a silent prayer. Grief is kept under control in public and proceedings are dignified. The body is transported in procession to the cemetery, vehicles often bearing large sprays of blue and white flowers. It is placed in the open grave with the head facing Mecca, the face cloth is removed, and planks are placed over it. Relatives sprinkle petals into the grave and, after further prayers, all present throw in a handful of soil. All witnesses remain until the grave is filled.

For Muslims, white is the traditional color of mourning, but wearing somber dress and a white armband is acceptable. Refreshments may be served before the ritual cleansing. Blue and white flowers may be sent to the home or a small gift of money may be given in a white envelope. (If sending flowers for any occasion, seek the florist's advice as to what is suitable.)

Dress Code for Ceremonies
Practice is changing, especially in Jakarta and larger cities and towns. Invitations to the various functions and *selamatan* will generally prescribe dress. Among the well-to-do, men will be expected to wear a suit. If no instructions are given and it is a neighborhood or village event, then men may

wear a long-sleeved shirt and tie or a long-sleeved batik shirt. As a general rule, dress conservatively. It would definitely be unsuitable for a man to wear shorts and sandals or for a woman to have bare arms, cleavage, and a short skirt. One lady at an official reception attended by the writer wore an expensive designer outfit that would have won accolades at Ascot but in the circumstances made her embarrassingly conspicuous.

If in Doubt, Ask!

Variations in practice occur between regions, between countryside and town, and between generations. If in doubt about protocol, not only about dress but regarding the size of gift or any other aspect of the occasion, do not be afraid to ask an Indonesian friend or colleague, who will appreciate your interest in the event and your concern to do the right thing. Being courteous, Indonesians will overlook any gaffe you may make, especially if they can see that you have made an effort, but good advice will prevent this.

Public *Selamatan*

The royal courts of Yogyakarta and Surakarta, whose rulers retained their positions if not their power because of their nationalist credentials, hold *selamatan* on special occasions. The largest and most popular, known as Sekatan and coinciding with the Prophet Mohammed's birthday, is a spectacular example of how Islam and Javanese tradition have blended. Thousands of visitors pour into these two cities to celebrate a monthlong carnival. The culmination is an elaborate and colorful procession through the streets in which courtiers, palace officials and guards, musicians, and dancers escort two mountains of rice and vegetables (*gunungan*), representing the ancient fertility symbols, the *lingga* (male) and the *yoni* (female), to the mosque, where they are blessed and the food distributed to the people. Eating it and placing a portion on the ground is said to ensure good health, fertility, and abundant harvests.

BALINESE CEREMONIES

It is practically impossible to avoid witnessing some aspect of Balinese ritual life during even a short stay in Bali. Apart from the performances put on for tourists, you may come across a procession, a celebration, or votaries offering gifts at a shrine.

Hinduism on Bali is distinctly Balinese, with pre-Hindu beliefs, spirits, and rituals incorporated into it. It is also capable of embracing new deities and forms of worship so that it remains a living system of belief, in the same way that Balinese art, drama, and dance subtly adapt without losing their distinctive style or becoming museum pieces.

Balinese life is guided by ritual. The religious calendar and observances structure the day, the year, and life itself. The traditional Balinese house

is itself a religious structure in which the family shrine to the ancestors has a central role. The "house" consists of a walled enclosure entered by a gateway consisting of two high pillars supporting a roof of thatch. In front, on either side of the gate, are two small shrines for offerings, while inside a short wall screens the interior and prevents evil spirits from entering. Family members live in pavilions around the common courtyard and share a common kitchen and the family temple, which houses the shrine to the ancestors and those to other deities. The arrangement of rooms and pavilions is dictated by concepts of hierarchy and auspicious location.

You Might Become the Guest of Honor!
If you are invited to attend a ceremony or festive occasion, even if you are a casual passerby, you may be treated as a guest of honor. Accept with dignity and enjoy the experience. Base your behavior on what you observe, bearing in mind the religious and cultural sensitivities of your hosts.

Balinese life is communal. Ritual is subsumed into daily living, within the home and in the village community. A village (*desa*) is itself divided into smaller cooperative neighborhood groups known as *banjar*, whose members are obliged to support each other during festivals, marriages, and funerals. Each *banjar* has a *bale* or communal hall, a drum tower from which meetings are called, a communal kitchen for preparing the feasts accompanying celebrations and performances, a *gamelan* orchestra and dance costumes, and a communal temple.

Funerals
The Balinese cremate their dead in elaborate and expensive ceremonies that may take place within a few days or as long as two years after a person's death. The delay enables a family to gather the money and other resources necessary for a

satisfactory funeral. In the meantime, the deceased's body is kept in the house, or if there is to be a long delay before the funeral it is mummified or buried temporarily.

After death, rituals are performed for a period of forty-two days to purify the body and to prepare the soul for its final separation from the mortal remains. Auspicious days are selected for these rituals and for the cremation, and a number of funerals may take place at the same time. The cremations are what you may see as a visitor. A person of high rank is placed in a coffin shaped like a bull if a man, like a cow if a woman. Other shapes are used for other ranks of society.

The evening before the funeral, after prayers at the family temple, relatives, guests, and villagers gather at the house. War dances are performed to ward off evil spirits, and the orchestras, including the *gambang*, only heard at funerals, play through the night. The night passes with a shadow play and readings from the *Bhima Swarga*, the Balinese classic recounting the adventures of Bhima, the epic Hindu hero, in the underworld.

On the day of the funeral, after preparations are complete and a final feast has been eaten, the body is taken from the house through or over the compound wall, not through the gate, and carried, twisting and turning with great commotion to confuse the corpse so that it cannot retrace its path and return to the house, to the brightly ornamented wooden and bamboo cremation tower waiting for it.

An uproarious procession of towers proceeds to the cemetery where the bodies are placed in their coffins while relatives crowd around. The high priest conducts the final rites before the fires are lit. The cremation is watched by the crowd while men stoke the fires and poke the bodies to help them burn. The noise from the crowd and the orchestras is neither solemn nor reverent. The body is no longer important since the

soul has left. As the sun sets and the light fades, the ashes are spread over the waters, and the people bathe to cleanse themselves and return to their homes.

Communal ritual and ceremony have a number of functions. The offerings, sacrifices, and prayers assist the passage of the soul to the spirit world and ensure that it will not return to haunt the living. They demonstrate respect for the dead and recognition of their place in the community when living. They also bind the community together and assure the bereaved of its support.

chapter four

INDONESIANS AT HOME

HOUSING

As anywhere, housing varies enormously, from the elaborate mansions of the wealthy to the crowded hovels of the poor; from the apartments and shophouses of the cities to the indigenous housing of many rural areas. In traditional societies in particular, status rather than wealth is important, though a person of status will generally have property and objects defining status. Very often the size of a house may reflect the size of the family rather than its wealth: on the other hand, small houses often contain surprisingly large families.

Traditional Indonesian housing is adapted to the climate, allowing the free circulation of air. Windows had shutters, which could be kept open for air and light, or shut to keep out direct sunlight or tropical windswept rain. Often these houses were built on stilts, again aiding the circulation of air and protection from local flooding, but also providing extra living and storage space. More modern housing, whether of concrete or brick, was also designed with verandas, large rooms, and, once electricity was available, ceiling fans. In the Chinatown areas of the old towns, the shophouses were built with air-wells. More recent housing designed with air-conditioning in mind will still in many cases provide a veranda or balcony for sitting out.

Expatriate Housing

Expatriates living and working in Jakarta reside in areas near the main business district or further out and to the south of the city center, near the Jakarta International School. These are areas with a mixed population of expatriates and middle- and upper-class Indonesians. Older houses may conform to the colonial pattern, with kitchens separate from the main house and bedrooms with external doors, but newer houses and apartments or renovated older houses follow  Western layouts. Employers usually provide housing for their expatriate staff and middle-class Indonesians have themselves adopted many aspects of Western design.

In most provincial cities, it will be possible to find houses adapted to Western living. Often smaller than in the expatriate areas of Jakarta, they will have attached kitchens and bathrooms and if used by previous expats will probably have installed Western plumbing, water heaters, baths, showers, and pedestal toilets: the amenities to which most Westerners are accustomed and to which many of the Indonesian middle classes aspire. Whether the systems always work may be another matter.

Jakarta and the other cities of Indonesia continue to grow at a rate that places a strain on public utilities. Check that your accommodation has water storage tanks and keep a store of flashlights (with batteries), kerosene lamps, and candles in reserve. Power outages may occur, especially during storms, so it is wise to protect sensitive equipment like computers and music systems from fluctuations and outages. Cooking is mainly done by gas.

The problems mentioned here should not be exaggerated. Employers and colleagues are aware of them so do not be afraid to seek advice from them. Your non-Indonesian colleagues have themselves experienced all these things and your Indonesian colleagues will wish you to settle in comfortably. In most cases all will proceed smoothly. For the rest, keep your sense of humor, get to know your neighbors, and adapt.

Bathrooms

Westerners in Indonesia are usually concerned about the quality of the plumbing, particularly the washing and bathroom facilities. The traditional method of washing is to use a container to pour over your body water stored in an open tank in the bathroom, the water draining away through a hole in the floor. Do not mistake the tank for a bath and get into it!

The traditional Indonesian lavatory is a squat toilet, with slightly raised footings on which to place your feet. There will also be a hook from which to hang your pants. There may not be toilet paper, but there will be a tap from which you may wash yourself before rising. As this requires the use of the left hand, you will recognize one reason for this hand being considered unclean. If there is toilet paper, there may be a small bin or container to place it in after use, to prevent it from blocking the plumbing. Most lavatories will have a flush system, but in others there will be a bucket or container to fill from the tap in order flush the pan, or there may be a length of hose.

Be Prepared

You may not encounter the need to use the traditional bathing and toilet facilities, but it is a wise precaution to carry toilet paper with you.

DAILY LIFE AND ROUTINE
The Air-conditioned Life

For expatriates, daily routine will not differ greatly from their normal experience, although you will find yourself having to adapt to the tropical climate and to the conditions it imposes. However, the prevalence of air-conditioning in housing, workplaces, shopping malls, hotels, and restaurants, especially in Jakarta and larger urban centers, has modified the climate's impact on daily life. It is now possible to live in an air-conditioned house, drive to an air-conditioned place of work in an air-conditioned car, eat in an air-conditioned restaurant, drink in an air-conditioned bar, and return, by air-conditioned car, to sleep in an air-conditioned bedroom. It is air-conditioning that enables you to retain your European wardrobe and for men to wear a suit in the office. You will be made clearly and uncomfortably aware of this should there be a power outage.

The Working Day

Nevertheless, most Indonesians have to adapt to the tropical climate. For many, "air-conditioning" continues to consist of open windows to allow a free flow of air and ceiling or desk fans. This means that the day begins relatively early, with government offices and commercial and business premises opening at 8:00 a.m. and closing at 4:00 p.m., although some commercial and business premises open from 9:00 a.m. to 5:00 p.m. In Jakarta and the larger cities, traffic conditions are such that many Indonesians will leave home before 6.00 a.m., often skipping breakfast and having a quick snack at work if there is a cafeteria or at a street store or coffee shop.

There is usually a midmorning break for a snack. Lunch is generally taken between 12:00 and 1:00 p.m. In smaller family-run stores you may see family members eating at the back of the shop. In the cities people flock to the food halls, usually in the basements of large buildings, sometimes at upper levels, where stalls sell a great variety of local and fast foods. These are crowded, noisy places, best visited after the lunch-hour rush or in the evenings. There are also off-the-street fast-food outlets and food stalls in a variety of venues. Laborers and outdoor workers may find a place to rest out of the sun.

At the end of the working day there is the return journey home, often preceded by a snack or cooling drink at a shop or stall. The evening meal is generally eaten at home, although food stalls are also well patronized, as people enjoy the cool of the evening. Workers retire early ready for the next day's early start.

Shopping

Indonesians have access to a wide range of shops, from department stores and specialized outlets in modern commercial complexes selling a huge range of foreign and locally produced goods, to humble general stores on the streets of all districts, selling a great variety of goods aimed at the local market. In Jakarta and the larger cities you will be able to find most of the items you are accustomed to, though not necessarily all the familiar brands. Supermarkets and department stores are fixed price and easy to shop in. They also give you an idea of the prices you may expect to pay when you wish to shop in the markets. It will take some time to become accustomed to the currency, but you will soon realize that for basic necessities prices are cheaper than you are used to.

There are also early morning fresh produce markets and night markets, both of which are fascinating places to visit, even if you do not buy anything. Stay long enough and you will realize that local shopkeepers operate a three-tier system of pricing—European (and other "wealthy" foreigners), general public, and friends. You will know that you have made it when you reach the third.

In the cities, and in Jakarta in particular, all kinds of goods, many produced in Indonesia, may be bought, from the latest electronic products to clothing, household goods, and furniture. If in Indonesia for the long term you can refurnish your house or apartment inexpensively and to your taste.

Made to Measure

This is the experience of an expatriate couple recently posted to Jakarta as teachers.

"We have bought most of our furniture here. It is so cheap and the quality is good. We had two large sofas made from pictures copied from the Internet . . . and have ordered a sofa bed. All our curtains and blinds have been made as well. You can get anything copied—just take the original or show a picture. Lots of tailors and shoemakers. It's just the traffic that is the problem . . . . Thankfully we have our driver, who is a perfect gentleman and is always there to pick us up when we need him."

Currency

The Indonesian currency is the rupiah (Rp). All major currencies in traveler's checks and cash are exchangeable in banks and exchange offices. Credit cards are accepted in larger hotels, businesses, and restaurants and in tourist areas. In local shops and remote areas you will need cash, much of it in small-denomination notes (Rp100, Rp500, and Rp1000) as getting change is difficult.

Business Hours

The following times may vary from place to place. Be aware that, even if government offices are open, the officials you have to deal with may not be available. It is advisable to visit government offices early in the morning if you are to complete your business within the day.

- Government offices are open from 8:00 a.m. until 4:00 p.m. Monday to Friday, with a break for prayers between 11:30 a.m. and 1:30 p.m. on Friday, and from 8:00 a.m. until 2:00 p.m. on Saturday.
- Post offices follow government hours, though smaller ones may close at 2:00 p.m.
- Commercial offices and businesses are usually open from 8:00 a.m. to 4:00 p.m. or from 9:00 a.m. to 5:00 p.m., with a variable lunch break of one hour. Some are open on Saturday morning.

- Muslim businesses close between 11:30 a.m. and 1:30 p.m. on Friday.
- Bank hours may vary slightly. Banks are usually open from 8:00 a.m. until 3:00 p.m. Monday to Friday and from 8:30 a.m. to 12:00 noon or 1:00 p.m. on Saturday.
- Moneychangers operate during normal shopping hours, which are variable.
- Shopping malls in the cities are open from 9:00 a.m. to 8:00 or 9:00 p.m. Some are also open on Sunday.
- Smaller shops usually open early in the morning and remain open until late at night, but times may vary at the owner's whim.
- Restaurants usually close at 11 p.m., but street stalls remain open until later.

THE FAMILY AND CHILDREN

Despite official attempts to limit family size, the family is the basis of Indonesian society. "Family" means the extended family. While modern life has placed great strains upon the extended family and among the younger generation in the cities the nuclear family may appear the norm, in reality links are maintained. Many city dwellers are recent arrivals or only a generation removed from rural villages and still have broad family obligations.

Children are wanted, loved, and indulged. Adults are tolerant of them and families are often seen together. The traditional method of carrying the child in a shoulder sling (*selendang*) encourages the bond between mother and child. As children grow, there is usually an adult around to see to their needs and to cuddle and care for them, whether it be a grandparent, an elder sibling, or a cousin or other relative brought in to provide care. If a mother is working, an *ayah* or *babu anak* (nanny) may be employed.

Once a child is approaching school age, they will be expected to take on simple household chores, to look after younger siblings, to show obedience and respect to their elders and to honor them, especially the father (*bapak*). Within the extended family a child will generally form a special bond with an elder member—uncle, aunt, cousin, or grandparent—and may even move to live in that person's household. They may also move between households. The bonds of family and of mutual responsibility are thus forged. With them come the obligations of the younger to the elder and the elder to the younger. Thus a young man will be expected both to care for his parents and to provide for his younger siblings.

Education is regarded as important for finding employment and for raising status. Educated children will be better able to look after their elders and provide for their younger siblings. Primary education is available to both sexes. About 88 percent of the Indonesian population over the age of fifteen can read and write, with the female literacy rate at about 84 percent trailing men only slightly. Education for all is in the national language, Bahasa Indonesia, which has been a major factor in creating a sense of national identity. Families make great efforts to ensure that their children attend school and Indonesia has a well-established educational system, from primary school to university.

Placing family before self has advantages in that one will always be looked after and have a roof over one's head—even if that roof may be that of different family members at different times. It also brings obligations like seeing to the welfare of the elderly in the family or financing the education of a junior member. Some may not marry whom and when they choose because of the family financial obligations they must continue to meet. On the other hand, one can always expect a helping hand when looking for a job, a promotion, or an opportunity from members of the family able to provide it. In the West we might call it nepotism, but it is also a form of social security.

Spoiled Kids
In modern Indonesia, the traditional view of family life is changing. Especially among the newly wealthy, one may find examples of indulged and undisciplined children, where the structures of the extended family have at least partially broken down.

It follows from the above that family celebrations feature prominently. The *selamatan* associated with many family occasions is described in Chapter 3. There are, however, other times when families will gather together to celebrate events such as educational success, business promotion, completion of a home addition, or just to ensure family goodwill and harmony. These will involve the recitation of prayers as well as a meal.

ENTERTAINING

Indonesians rarely entertain formally, though this is changing with some of the new middle and professional classes. An expatriate working with Indonesians may be invited to a restaurant along with other expatriate and Indonesian colleagues and friends of the host. Business functions may also bring people together as a group to eat and drink, but the stand-up reception or cocktail party format is not usual. Indonesians prefer to sit down to eat and the Islamic proscription against alcohol is also a factor. Moreover, while many Indonesians working with expatriates are fluent in English, their spouses and friends may not be. Conversation can be stilted and limited. With a carefully devised seating plan, this type of embarrassment can be avoided.

Bear these thoughts in mind when entertaining Indonesian friends. Welcome them with a selection of chilled nonalcoholic drinks accompanied by nuts and other local snacks taken around and offered on small plates. The meal itself should be served buffet style, but places at the table should have name cards. Invite the most prominent person present to head the line and explain the contents of the dishes, remembering to assure your Muslim guests that what you serve is *halal.* After the meal, tea and coffee may be served in the sitting room. Indonesians regard coffee as ending both the meal and the evening and will then shortly begin to depart, usually awaiting the first move from the most prominent guest.

HOUSEHOLD HELP

Entertaining is relatively easy for expatriate residents because there will be household help, as there is for Indonesians who can afford it. It is usual to acquire one or more servants, depending on the size of your accommodation and on your lifestyle. You are expected to have domestic staff, which may extend to a gardener and a driver. A single person or a couple in an apartment may manage with one servant, who may live in or come in daily and when required. Families may also acquire someone to help look after the children.

If you plan to stay a while in Indonesia, seek advice from your colleagues before employing anyone. They will have been through the process and will probably be able to suggest suitable candidates. You may inherit an employee who worked for your predecessor. Word will soon get around that you are looking and the servants of your colleagues will hear of it. Take a little time before making a decision. Seek testimonials and have with you, when you interview candidates, a person with some experience in employing household staff and some knowledge of the language.

Conditions of service, including the amount of free time and the level of wages, should be commensurate with those of servants employed by your colleagues.

Servants should be clear as to what is expected of them. At the same time, employers should be aware that their staff have expectations as well and have to be treated with respect. As in all relationships in Indonesia, confrontation should be avoided and agreement reached by discussion and agreement. Servants understand their role and will respond more willingly to clear direction and guidance than to direct orders. Nevertheless, the employer–servant relationship is a personal one and different individuals will develop different relationships with their staff. Treat them fairly and with consideration, while making clear your expectations.

TIME OUT

INDONESIANS AND LEISURE

The concept of leisure in the Western sense is
alien to most Indonesians. Those who have had
contact with Westerners do pursue "leisure
activities," that is, they play sport (and watch it),
exercise, shop for pleasure, go to the beach, have
picnics, attend cinemas, concerts, and dramatic
performances, eat out,
entertain, and so on. For
most Indonesians,
however, leisure is less
packaged. It is time
when one is not
working and much of
that time is with the

family. Families will be seen in the cool of the
evening at the food stalls, chatting, relaxing,
walking in small groups, meeting friends. Sport is
likely to be a casual affair—football, basketball,
badminton, or traditional games—played in the
evening by young men on a patch of ground.
Television is popular and many households watch

regularly. There are still traditional activities ranging from kite flying to cock fighting. In many areas there will be traditional performances of dance and drama. Leisure activities are as varied as the population.

SHOPPING FOR PLEASURE

As a visitor you may well be tempted to buy traditional arts and crafts as souvenirs, or even decide to have something produced locally and sent to your home. Foreign residents, too, are attracted to Indonesian products and artifacts. These are obtainable in fixed-price shops, but you may wish to explore further in nonfixed-price shops, bazaars, and markets, in which case be prepared to bargain.

Bargaining

Bargaining is part of the shopping experience, but some discretion is necessary. Much depends on the shopper's own attitude—which is to bargain confidently and with a smile. In smaller shops ask for a discount or a rounding down of the bill. If you do not get an actual discount, you may get a little bit extra of what you are purchasing—so there is no harm in asking. Be nice about it—part of the reward for the shopkeeper is seeing the pleasure of someone they like with a "bargain."

Equally, there is pleasure in overcharging or denying a discount to a customer who is unpleasant and impolite.

Bargaining is usually the rule at street stalls selling merchandise other than food. If quoted a price, offer about half or a little more of the asking price. The seller will lower his price and you should raise your offer. After perhaps ten minutes or more, during which you examine the desired article and others on the stall, talk generally of other matters, and show no desperate need or desire for the item, you and the seller should meet at a point some 10 percent (or, hopefully, more) lower than the original asking price. The final ploy in the bargaining process is to indicate regret and walk away. The chances are that the seller will follow and accept your offer. It is important to remember that once you or the seller has accepted the other's price the deal has been settled.

Indonesian Textiles
Indonesia is famous for its traditional textiles. In particular look for:

Batik
Molten wax is applied to fabric to prevent dye penetrating the cloth, those portions of the fabric free of wax accepting the dye. By repeating the

process many times, complex multicolored patterns can be produced. The most famous batik centers are Surakarta and Yogyakarta in central Java and Pekalongan in northern Java.

Ikat
The threads are tied and dyed before weaving, producing attractive designs with slightly blurred outlines. Ikat is produced in many parts of Indonesia including Java, Sumatra, Bali, Sulawesi, Kalimantan, and Nusa Tenggara.

Songket
Patterns and motifs are woven into the cloth with gold and silver thread. Sumatra and Bali are important areas of production.

Barkcloth
Produced in the highland areas of Kalimantan, Sulawesi, and Irian Jaya, it is made by pulping the bark of suitable plants and beating it into sheets, which are then decorated.

Arts and Crafts
Indonesia is renowned for high-quality craft work in a wide range of regional styles. Look for pottery

and basketwork, wood carving and metalwork. Very distinctive is the ceremonial dagger or *kris*, which varies in design of both hilt and blade in different parts of Indonesia. Stone carving is a feature in particular of Bali, which also produces the more elaborate form of *kris*. Modern wood carving is well developed in Java and Bali. More "primitive" styles are produced in Kalimantan, Sulawesi, and Irian Jaya.

Bali is famous for its art and for the colonies of Indonesian and foreign artists, attracted by the culture, the climate, and the people. The artistic center is the inland town of Ubud with its numerous galleries with work for sale. Yogyakarta on Java has a similar reputation. In both places look also for the leather puppets that are used in the *wayang* or shadow play.

Jewelry, mainly of silver and semiprecious stones, is widely produced, with Bali an important center. Unless you are reasonably expert, it is best to buy from reputable stores attached to the hotels.

Antiques

Genuine antiques are expensive and it is best to buy from well established shops. There are laws forbidding the export of antiques that have come from an archaeological site. There is a thriving industry making fake "antiques"—amulets, carvings, ceramics, artifacts, fabrics, beads, and other items are made and then "aged" for the tourist market. They make attractive and interesting souvenirs, and occasionally one may be lucky enough to find a genuine antique, but do not place much trust in guarantees of their provenance, unless from a reputable source.

Touts and Scalpers
Usually these are young men who receive a commission from a shop, hotel, restaurant, or taxi/bus company. They often have good English and are knowledgeable. Generally, they are best ignored as politely as possible. On the lookout for tourists, they will soon recognize you and ignore you if you are resident for any length of time, although you will find them elsewhere if you travel. Once you have a few words of Indonesian you can persuade them of your familiarity with the country.

SPORTS AND GAMES
Western sports and games have been introduced into the country. Traditional Indonesian sports include kite flying, top spinning, and games using a light ball made of woven rattan; bull racing takes place in Madura and East Java. These days sports such as badminton, basketball, and soccer are popular, largely because they do not need elaborate

facilities, can be played on any patch of ground, and are shown on television. Snooker tables may be found in some bazaars. Wealthier Indonesians may play tennis, squash, and golf, games that require larger courts or extensive space. Amongst the younger generation, computer games are popular.

Sports and games have played an important role in expatriate life since colonial times. The climate places restrictions on physical activity, but today outdoor lighting and air-conditioning extend the possibilities. Old hands will tell you that there is nothing like getting up a good sweat before replacing water loss with something refreshing from the cold box or bar.

HASH HOUSE HARRIERS (H3)

This running club began in Kuala Lumpur in 1938 and was revived after the Second World War. The name derives from an eating house at which young expatriate men, after a Monday evening run, met to recoup their strength and replace water loss with the local beer. After a time, the run was started from different locations and became a paper chase. Popular among the expatriate community throughout Southeast Asia (there are runs for women and for children), it is to be found in Indonesia and, for something different, is worth seeking out.

Providing one is sensible and takes in adequate water to prevent dehydration, one can play most sports. Foreign companies often have their own facilities, squash, badminton, and tennis being popular, as well as soccer, field hockey, and golf. Some clubs and teams also provide social facilities.

NIGHTLIFE

Nightlife in the Western sense is confined to the bigger cities. There are nightclubs, restaurants, bars, theaters, and cinemas, but for most Indonesians the main evening pleasure is eating out, the wealthier at restaurants, most people at street stalls. The large hotels are popular with the well-to-do. Western-style fast-food restaurants attract the younger set. Families commonly eat together and children will eat with their elders at restaurants and street stalls well into the evening.

Wayang (traditional theater performed by actors and dancers or puppets) is popular and performances are frequent in towns and villages. Different areas have their own variations, but it is particularly strong in Java and Bali. Tourist areas have a wide variety of performances, many of them in the hotels, but others in more public places at which Indonesians will also gather. On Bali there are performances of dance and drama associated with the temples and festivals.

FOOD AND DRINK

There is a wide range of cuisines in Indonesia, all worth trying. Follow the advice of colleagues until you have become acclimatized and have adjusted to the unfamiliar, generally spicy, flavors.

Many Indonesians are familiar with Western customs and tourist and business hotels provide Western-style tableware and menus. If you are invited to an Indonesian home, however, or as a guest to an Indonesian restaurant, you should be aware of basic Indonesian etiquette.

Dining Etiquette

Before you start the meal your host may direct you to a basin to wash your hands or provide you with scented water and a towel. Finger bowls will be placed on the table if you are expected to use your fingers. If you do, then wash your hands again at the end of the meal.

Indonesians usually use a spoon and a fork. In Indonesian cuisine, meat and vegetables are cut small before cooking and are served with rice and a spicy sauce on plates or in bowls on a table or, in humbler dwellings, on a mat on the floor.

It is good manners to take small portions onto your own plate or bowl: take extra small helpings during the course of the meal rather than load your plate at the outset.

You may eat certain foods with your right hand (remember that the left hand is unclean): take your cue from your hosts and the other guests.

Finger Food

If required to eat with your fingers remember that only the right hand may be used and the food is taken with your fingertips. It requires some skill, but your hosts will appreciate your efforts, and a spoon will appear if you need it.

When you have eaten enough, move any uneaten food to one side of your plate. It is good manners to leave something on your plate to show that you have been fully fed. Place your spoon and fork parallel on the plate, face downward.

Toothpicks are usually on the table. If you need to use one, cover your mouth with your free hand.

During the meal, you will probably be offered water (often warm, to indicate that it has been boiled), tea, or bottled mineral water. You will not usually be offered alcohol, although you may be in non-Muslim households and it will be available in tourist hotels and restaurants. Alcohol is served in Bali and other non-Muslim areas.

Don't Clear Your Plate!

A new arrival was invited home by an Indonesian colleague. The food was to his taste, he cleared his plate, and was offered more. Again he cleared his plate, assuming that by so doing he was showing his appreciation. Again more food was placed on his plate. Eventually, he could not finish and his plate was removed, his hosts commenting on his capacity, the visitor feeling very uncomfortable internally for the rest of the evening.

Indonesians do not linger over their meals. The food is usually eaten in silence, with little talking, after which it is usual to retire to a lounge area. There, conversation will continue until it is time to leave. The most senior or important guest takes leave first, after which other guests gradually depart, with thanks to their hosts. As in all communities, once you have established friendships, etiquette is relaxed. However, it is always best to err on the side of formality until relationships have been defined and accepted.

The business traveler or expatriate employee may well have cocktail party-type functions to attend, with canapés and Indonesian-style tidbits (*makan kechil*). Depending on the occasion and the hosts, alcohol may or may not be served, and it is wise to observe what others are drinking before asking for something stronger than fruit juice or a soft drink. Small items like nuts may be taken into the left hand, preferably on a napkin, and then eaten with the right.

Eating Out

Hotel restaurants and bars are expensive, but there are plenty of other eating and drinking establishments. In expatriate and tourist areas there will be some member of staff who can speak English and menus may be in English.

Restoran Padang offer a style of eating originally from Padang in Sumatra. They are common everywhere. There is no menu. Customers are offered a plate of plain rice and small dishes of spicy meat, fish, and vegetables are brought to the table. You pay only for what you eat.

Small eating houses, often called *rumah makan*, *warung*, or even *restoran*, are common. The simplest serve a limited range of food. They may display a menu board. If not, ask what there is or observe what others are eating.

Chinese restaurants are found throughout the country. They tend to be slightly more expensive than Indonesian restaurants.

Street vendors may carry food and a cooking pot suspended from a pole on their shoulders. More common is a man with a barrow that has a stove and food in a glass cabinet on top. Others have a fixed site with a stall, often with a table and stools nearby. Street vendors usually sell rice dishes, noodles, soup, *sate* (meat, usually small pieces of chicken, on skewers, cooked over charcoal), ice-cream and *rujak,* a mixed fruit salad with chilli and peanuts.

It is safe to eat at both restaurants and food stalls: the food is well cooked. But it is advisable to drink only bottled water, or drinks such as tea or coffee prepared with boiled water.

Drinks

Imported beers and spirits are available in many restaurants and bars, but wine is less common. Muslim restaurants may not serve alcohol, but local beer is widely available and is worth trying. Long drinks such as  gin and tonic or brandy and ginger ale suit the climate and there are fruit-based and soft drinks for those who do not want alcohol. Expatriates in the tropics have invented a number of nonalcoholic drinks using soda water, dry ginger ale, or bitters mixed with lemon or lime juice, or another fruit drink.

TIPPING

Tipping was not a general practice, but has come to be expected. The expensive hotels and restaurants normally add 21 percent to the bill to cover service and tax. Elsewhere 10 percent is appropriate, or change may be left.

Street vendors and stallholders do not normally expect tips, but will be happy to hear the words *simpaniah sisanah*, meaning "Keep the change." Hotel porters expect about Rp500 per bag. Taxi drivers expect the fare to be rounded up to the nearest Rp500 or Rp1,000. Hire-car drivers expect a tip at the end of the journey.

Bear in mind that, given the value of the rupiah, these sums are not unreasonable. You will soon become used to treating apparently large sums of money as small change

chapter **six**

TRAVEL, HEALTH, & SAFETY

ROAD TRAVEL
Cars
Tourists and business travelers may find their
transportation needs largely catered for by their
tour operators or business hosts. Visitors may
also hire a car with a driver, a self-drive car, or
a motorcycle. Traffic drives on the left, the
maximum speed limit is 60 kph (45 mph),
and you need to carry with you at all times
your international
driver's license and
the registration
documents of the
vehicle. Motorcyclists
must wear helmets.

While all this appears
straightforward,
driving in most places
is not. The roads are
crowded, especially in
and near the larger

cities. Whatever the law may say, the size and weight of vehicle often determines right of way. While there are good highways, including toll roads, driving on them is often fast and erratic. Other roads may be in poor repair and carry traffic of all shapes and sizes, much of it overcrowded and overloaded.

If you are working in Indonesia, a car may be useful for regular journeys between home and work. Many expatriates employ a driver, or their employer may provide one. If you are a visitor going on longer journeys, hiring a car and driver reduces the stress. Before you start, negotiate the trip and the time you wish to take. You will be expected to pay for the driver's meals and accommodation, but the costs are reasonable.

Taxis

Taxis operate in the cities and towns. In Jakarta and the larger towns they are metered: but check that the meter is on. Elsewhere be prepared to bargain. If you are staying in a place for a few days and you are satisfied with your driver, be prepared to bargain for his services for the duration of your stay. This is usually an advantageous arrangement for both of you.

Intercity taxis and minibuses are convenient ways of traveling between nearby cities.

> **Don't Forget…**
> Always carry with you the written details of your
> destination, with directions if you can obtain
> them, the address of where you live or are staying,
> and the relevant telephone numbers.

Bajaj and *Becak*

For short distances the *bajaj*, a three-wheeled
motorized vehicle, will whisk you noisily through

the city traffic, or you may
try a bicycle rickshaw
(trishaw) known as a
becak. This can be a
nerve-racking
experience in heavy
traffic, but at quieter

times and in the evening can be a leisurely and
pleasant way of getting around. If in a place for an
extended period, it is advisable to employ the
same *becak* and settle on the price beforehand. On
first use, be prepared to bargain.

Buses

For the adventurous, local bus services are usually
crowded and uncomfortable, but they are cheap
and are certainly a way to meet the locals. Luggage
is tied to the roof under a tarpaulin, so take on to
the bus anything you may need on the journey.

If possible, board at the bus station so that you can choose a seat. (Jakarta has more than one bus station, so check which one you need.) Buses tend to fill up from the rear so do not be alarmed if someone squeezes in next to you when there are empty seats still available in front. Indonesians are generally smaller than Europeans so three will squeeze into a space for two, and a European may well lack legroom. Though you may be squashed, your fellow passengers will almost certainly be friendly and also intrigued by your presence. If you are prepared to respond—and why travel by bus otherwise—you will have a memorable and enjoyable journey.

Minibuses, often converted vans or trucks, are found everywhere under various names—*bemos, colts, microlets, oplets.* These are cheap, but crowded.

Long-distance express buses, often air-conditioned and comfortable, operate between cities and, via ferry services, between islands. Night express buses (*bis malam*) also operate between certain cities. In some places, such as between Surakarta and Yogyakarta, express buses run at regular intervals and drop you at your hotel or guesthouse (*losman*) if asked.

Privately owned tourist buses operate in and between tourist areas. They are convenient and comfortable, but relatively expensive.

RAIL TRAVEL

Rail services operate on Java and parts of Sumatra. Most visitors will probably use the Java services. There are three classes of travel: first class, with air-conditioning, which may not be working; second class, with fans; and third class. Some overnight express trains have sleepers and reclining seats.

Best Laid Plans . . .

Not everything goes to plan. My wife and I, traveling with a young child, booked first-class tickets through a tourist office to travel on the night sleeper service of the Bima Express between Jakarta and Yogyakarta. We arrived, pushed through to the train, and were finally deposited in a crowded carriage with fans, piles of luggage in baskets, carrier bags, and a brace of trussed fighting cocks. We were informed that the air-conditioned sleeper service was not in operation. It was a hot, humid evening after a very hot, humid Jakarta day and the child was restless. I confess that we chickened out and the next day went by minibus to the cool of Bandung.

Tickets must be bought at the point of and on the day of departure, although some night express tickets may be bought a day in advance. If you are working in Indonesia, your office will probably have a messenger or other means of obtaining tickets for you. Visitors may prefer to pay extra through a tourist office rather than face the chaos often encountered at the railway station.

BOATS AND FERRIES

The national shipping line PELNI operates services throughout the archipelago. The larger ships offer first-class (en suite cabins with TV), second-class, and economy passages at reasonable prices.

Vehicle ferries operate between the main islands. Smaller islands are served by small craft of various kinds, often overloaded and of dubious seaworthiness. Thousands of journeys are made without mishap, however, and as there is often no other option, at least the journey will be memorable.

River transport is still the only option in many places, particularly in Kalimantan. River craft vary in size, speed, and comfort, but often operate regular services. For a long trip upriver take a sleeping mat, food, and bottled water. Some boats have kitchens or may stop for meals at riverside bazaars, but the variety of food decreases the further one penetrates the interior. There may be basic accommodation on land at night.

AIR TRAVEL

There are flights between the main centers of population and services are safe and generally reliable. Internal airfares are reasonable, with concessions for children up to twelve years. However, remember to confirm your booked flights 24 to 72 hours in advance at each stop. Flights can be overbooked, canceled, or delayed. In practice, except for return tickets, you need to be actually in a place before you can book a ticket out of it! Be prepared for delays and allow for them in your planning.

Garuda, the Indonesian national airline, offers a Visit Indonesia Air Pass to those entering the country on Garuda.

BETTER TO TRAVEL HOPEFULLY . . .

Tales of dire journeys should not deter you. Indonesian colleagues and friends will know the best ways to travel and may have useful contacts. They will probably attempt to warn you against going too far off the beaten path, as many will have had little experience of such travel themselves. Among expatriate colleagues there may be some who can give you the benefit of their experience. And there are publications and Web sites that cater specifically to the independent traveler.

HEALTH

As a visitor you will have few immunities to even relatively mild local diseases and ailments. Take the relevant precautions and make sure that you have adequate medical insurance as part of your employment or travel package.

Inoculations

No inoculations are legally required before you enter Indonesia unless you come from a country that has yellow fever, in which case you must have a certificate of immunization.

If you are traveling out of the main tourist and urban areas, inoculations are advisable for typhoid, tetanus, polio, and hepatitis A. For certain areas, inoculation against hepatitis B, rabies, and Japanese encephalitis may also be advisable. Your prospective employer should advise you, but consult your doctor and travel agent well in advance, too, as some inoculations may require a series of injections over time.

Malaria

Malaria is endemic and requires a program of drugs beginning at least a week before your departure and continuing for up to four weeks after  your return. The drug prescribed will depend upon the area to which you are going because certain strains of malaria resist some drugs. Consult your doctor well in advance. Carry mosquito repellent or purchase some immediately upon your arrival.

Intestinal Disorders

Most new arrivals experience some diarrhea if only because of the change in diet and climate. It will pass and nothing serious will eventuate if you take precautions. Carry a supply of tablets to use at the first signs of discomfort. Pharmacies in Indonesia carry several brands. Drink plenty of fluid to avoid dehydration. Pharmacies also carry rehydration salts.

Drinking Water

Tap water is unsafe throughout Indonesia. Drink only bottled mineral water (*air mineral*), which is available almost everywhere, or water that has been boiled for at least five minutes or has been filtered and chemically sterilized. Avoid ice in your drinks unless sure it is from a clean source. Drinks made with boiling water are safe, as are beer and brand-name mixes and soft drinks.

Sun Exposure

Because of the humidity, it is easy to underestimate the power of the sun. Cover up, wear a hat, use sunscreen, and take fluid and extra salt to counteract sweating. Avoid the sun during the hottest part of the day.

MEDICAL CARE

The major cities and tourist areas have reasonable medical facilities. If you are working, your employer will almost certainly have arrangements with a reliable doctor and clinic. If you are a tourist or on a short business trip, hotels usually have a doctor on call or can put you in touch with one. Elsewhere, medical facilities vary and many have limited resources. Most towns have well-stocked pharmacies at which you can buy a wide range of medicines and drugs. It is advisable to carry sufficient quantities of any medicines you use regularly.

SAFETY

Before traveling to Indonesia seek information about the situation in the areas you will be visiting. The Western media tends to emphasize the negative: that millions of Indonesians live peaceful lives is usually ignored. Where possible consult employers, business associates, and people with current experience. Situations can change but, on the whole, Indonesia is no more dangerous than any other country. There is tension in the province of Aceh, where a separatist movement exists, and elsewhere. However, most of this vast archipelago is safe for work and travel. Any embassy or travel agent will be able to advise you and potentially dangerous regions can be avoided. There remains a lot of Indonesia to visit.

Once in Indonesia, make sure that you have separate copies of your passport and all your travel documentation, and the telephone numbers of your credit card companies and your insurers. If working here you will have contact numbers and support from your employer and, increasingly as time goes by, from a network of friends. Carry a contact number and address with you. Take the precautions that you would at home to protect your billfold or purse while on the streets, shopping, or dining. Ascertain which areas of town are potentially dangerous, particularly after dark.

Common sense will keep you out of trouble as it does at home. In Indonesia, the great majority of people are friendly, helpful, courteous to strangers, and no threat. Learn at least some basic Indonesian phrases and courtesies—it helps establish a rapport.

PLACES TO VISIT
On Java, In and Around Jakarta
In Jakarta the Old Harbor (known as Sunda Kelapa), with its 1.2 mile (2 km) wharf, built in

1817, is still used by traditional sailing craft. There is also a nineteenth-century Dutch lookout tower. Nearby, the Museum Bahari, housed in a mid-seventeenth century Dutch warehouse, displays Indonesian trading vessels from throughout the archipelago. Little remains of Old Batavia, but three colonial buildings on Taman Fatahillah house the Jakarta History Museum, the Fine Arts Museum, and the Wayang Museum. A few other colonial buildings remain, as does Jakarta's bustling old Chinatown.

In central Jakarta are the Sukarno-era National Monument in Medan Merdeka (Freedom Square) and the Irian Jaya Freedom Memorial in the center of Lapangan Banteng (Wild Ox Field), which has also the National Cathedral (1901) and the Supreme Court (1848). Nearby stands the vast Istqial Mosque, built in white marble and the

largest in the region. On the western side of
Medan Merdeka, the National Museum houses a
huge collection of artifacts and treasures.

If you do not have time to travel further in
Indonesia, Taman Mini will give you a taste of the
whole country. About 6 miles (10 km) south of
Jakarta, this site encompasses 247 acres (100 ha)
and twenty-seven pavilions representing the
twenty-seven provinces of Indonesia, clustered
around a lake featuring a three-dimensional relief
map of the archipelago. In addition there are over
thirty other attractions including a Museum
Indonesia, a one-quarter scale replica of
Borobudur, a tropical bird park, and an orchid
garden. On Sundays dance and dramatic
performances attract large crowds. During the
week it is very quiet; some pavilions may not be
open, and it is worth checking in advance.

On Java, Away From Jakarta
Java may be a crowded island but it also boasts
spectacular scenery and a fascinating history and
culture. Within easy reach of Jakarta lies the
pleasant hill city of Bandung, which offers escape
from the heat of the capital. Cirebon on the north
coast has much of interest: its two palaces or
kraton dating from 1678 and the Grand Mosque
(Mesjid Ageng) from c. 1500. Nearby are villages
of artists and artisans. Pekalongan, 130 miles

(220 km) east of Cirebon, is famous for its batiks.
Semarang has an extensive old Chinatown, while
nearby is the hill retreat of Bandungan and the
eighth-century Hindu temples at Gedung Songo,
built on a spectacular mountain site and
dedicated to Siva.

Central Java is renowned for the temple of
Borobudur and the two cities of Yogyakarta and
Surakarta, each a center of traditional Javanese
culture, their courts keeping alive the ancient
traditions in music, dance, and drama.
Yogyakarta, with its proximity to Borobudur, is
better-known, but Surakarta still retains much of
the feel of the old city and royal court.

Bali

Those looking for sun, sand, shopping, and
nightlife head for Kuta, those with more sedate

tastes to Sanur, both on the southern coast, but the whole island has much to offer. Access is through the airport at Denpasar, the capital, or by ferry from Surabaya on Java.

Inland lies Ubud, a center for Balinese and foreign artists, set in beautiful hill country with spectacular rice terraces, the surrounding villages specializing in various crafts and art forms. The temple of Pura Alan Danu is perched on a crater rim, and at Kintamani, further around the crater, a market is held every three days.

Gunung Agung, on the eastern side of the island, is the most sacred of Bali's mountains. Traveling from the south, all roads pass through Gianyar, the weaving center of Bali, to Klungkung, the site of Bali's most important kingdom, noted for the eighteenth-century Kerta Gasa or Hall of Justice with its ceiling murals and the Bale Kambang or floating pavilion. North of Klungkung is the Pura Besakih, Bali's holiest shrine, a complex

of twenty-two temples on the lower slopes of Gunung Agung. Near Amlapura are the palaces and hydraulic creations of the last king of what was then called Karangasem.

Lombok

Lombok is the main island of the province of Nusa Tenggara Barat, with its capital Mataram. There are interesting cultural and architectural attractions within easy reach of Cakranegara, the old royal capital. These include the Pra Meru temple and the Pura Mayura royal gardens. Other temples and impressive views are at Mount Pengsong and Batu Balong. At Narmada is a nineteenth-century palace and garden built by the Balinese king of Karangasem. Lombok has also developed beach facilities on its south coast and offshore islands. Tetebatu and Sapit are peaceful mountain resorts. Gunung Rinjani, Indonesia's third largest mountain, may be climbed. Less testing is the climb to the beautiful crater lake of Segara Anak.

On Komodo, between the islands of Sumbawa and Flores, the largest monitor lizard in the world has become a tourist attraction.

Ende, on Flores, is capital of the province of Nusa Tenggara Timur. The mountain of Kreli Mutu in southern Flores has three crater lakes, which change color for no apparent reason. Sumba is off the beaten path but once a year attracts some visitors to its annual Pasola ceremony, during which ritual fights take place between groups of armed horsemen in the days following the full moon of the third lunar month.

Sumatra

Northwest of Java, it is the world's sixth largest island. Most visitors fly into Medan to visit the Batak Highlands and Lake Toba (Danau Toba), the largest lake in Southeast Asia, within the crater of an ancient volcanic eruption. Visit for the mountain scenery, cool climate, and picturesque Batak villages.

The Minangkabau region of West Sumatra, running inland from Padang on the coast to the hill station at Bukittinggi, is another region of spectacular natural beauty and cultural significance. The Minangkabau are remarkable for being staunch Muslims while retaining their traditional matrilineal society.

Palembang, on the east coast, retains no great architectural monuments. However, the Rumah Bari Museum contains megalithic, Hindu, and Buddhist statuary, while the music and dance display forms date back to the seventh century.

Bengkulu, on the southwest coast, was once a British trading station and Fort Marlborough, constructed in 1762, still stands. Sir Thomas Stamford Raffles, founder of Singapore, was Lieutenant-Governor from 1818 to 1823. The

Dendam Taksuda Botanical Gardens contain the giant Rafflesia flower named after him.

Aceh, with its capital Banda Aceh, was the first Southeast Asian state to accept Islam, in the fourteenth century. It retains a strong sense of identity and is currently suffering the ravages of the 2004 tsunami.

Sulawesi

Ujang Padang was once known as Makassar, the capital of the commercial empire of the Bugis until the Dutch captured it. Fort Rotterdam is now a museum, but Bugis boats still dock at Paotere.

Inland from Parepare is the land of the Toraja, a mainly Christian people who have retained their distinctive boat-shaped houses and unusual, complex funeral ceremonies, sometimes taking place years after death. These last for up to a week and are performed mainly during July and August, but also in May and June, at which time there are fewer tourists. Life-sized effigies of the dead are placed in cliff-side galleries high above the plain. The main center is Rantepao. The area provides enjoyable walking and good local transportation.

Central Sulawesi is difficult to access. The main attractions are the Bada Valley with its large stone megaliths, Lake Poso, and the Lore Lindu National Park.

North Sulawesi is more accessible, with direct flights to Manado from Singapore. Attractions include the Bunaken-Manado Marine National Park, which offers superb diving and snorkeling; the Tangkoko Batuangus National Park, Lake Tonando, and the Tamen Anggrek Orchid Garden at Airmaddi.

Maluku

Once known as the Moluccas, Maluku has great natural beauty and numerous relics of its colonial past. The island of Ambon is largely Christian. Kota Ambon, the administrative center for the region, was founded by the Portuguese in 1574 and then taken by the Dutch. Colonial remnants survive, including Fort Victoria and the residence of the Dutch governor. The Museum Siwalima houses tribal artifacts and other items.

The Banda Islands have old Dutch forts, beaches, reefs, and Mount Api to explore. Ternate and Tidore are two volcanic cones rising some 5,400 ft (1,700 m) from the sea about half a mile apart. Portuguese, Spanish, Dutch, and, briefly, English traded and competed with the native sultans for control of the spice trade, and fortifications litter the coast. The Kedaton in

Ternate, the palace of the last sultan, is now a museum. The islands offer diving, snorkeling, walking, climbing, and spectacular scenery.

Kalimantan (Borneo)

This territory is divided into three provinces: Kalimantan Barat (capital, Pontianak); Kalimantan Tengah (capital, Banjarmasin); and Kalimantan Timur (capital, Balikpapan).

Kalimantan is sparsely populated. The coastal areas are swampy so the few main cities are many miles inland on the banks of the major rivers, on the sites of early Muslim sultanates. These are inhabited mainly by Malays and Chinese. Resettlement schemes have introduced thousands of Javanese and Balinese peasants with varying success. The interior is inhabited by Dayak peoples whose traditional way of life is under pressure. Kalimantan supplies most of Indonesia's oil and timber and the exploitation of its resources is poorly controlled.

Pontianak offers access to the Kapuas River. A road links it to Singkawan, which has good beaches and Chinese temples, and to Sambas, known for its fine cloth. The Mandor National Park has a botanical garden, war memorial, and orchid gardens.

Banjarmasin, 13 miles (22 km) up the Barito River, built on a network of rivers and canals, is the center of the Indonesian gem trade. Of interest are the Sabilia Muhtadin Mosque, the early morning floating market, the old harbor (Pelabuhan Lama), and the Ceramic Museum.

Within reach of Banjarmasin are the National Parks of Pulau Keget, with proboscis monkeys, and the Pleihari Martapura, an orangutan reserve.

Balikpapan is an oil town. Samarinda, 40 miles (69 km) up the Mahakam River, can be reached from Balikpapan by road and river. More interesting than either of these is Tenggorong, onetime capital of the Sultan of Kutei. The palace is now the Mulawarman Museum, housing ceramics, royal regalia, and Dayak artifacts. From Tenggorong trips are organized up the Mahakam to Dayak country.

Irian Jaya

Irian Jaya (capital Jayapura) is Indonesia's largest province. Mountainous and sparsely populated, its interior was until recently largely untouched by the outside world. Travel is restricted, although Jayapura (once Hollandia) has some interest. For a time it was General MacArthur's Pacific Headquarters and the wreckage of several wartime vessels may be seen on the beaches of Yotefu National Park, east of Jayapura. The

Anthropological Museum at Cendrawasih University in Abepura, near Jayapura, has a collection of Irianese tribal artifacts, including prized Asmani carvings. Wamena, in the Baliem Valley in the highlands and home of the Dani people, is accessible by air from Jayapura. Agats, on the south coast, is open to tourists. The Museum of Culture and Progress displays Asmat carving and upriver trips may be arranged.

STAYING SAFE

There have been disturbances between Muslims and Christians on Ambon in Maluku, the post-tsunami truce in Aceh remains fragile at the time of writing, and the situation in Irian Jaya is also uncertain. Seek advice before planning to visit these areas, particularly if you wish to go outside the main cities. However, also remember that Indonesia covers a vast extent of territory, most of it untroubled and safe.

BUSINESS BRIEFING

Underlying business relations in Indonesia are the traditional family and communal attitudes governing Indonesian society. These operate in two ways. First, Indonesians believe in the importance of maintaining social harmony, which is dependent upon the inner spiritual harmony of individuals and regard for the feelings of others. Second, Indonesians believe in consensus. In private life this means reaching unanimous agreement after consultation with family, friends, and colleagues. In public life and business there is a similar striving for consensus, which may take numerous meetings and, to a Westerner, an inordinate amount of time.

PATRON/CLIENT RELATIONSHIPS

In the family, relations between individuals are defined by their relative position in the family structure. In business, professional, and political life, relations are defined by personal relations within the hierarchy, which may be based on family or regional ties, or upon personal obligations for services rendered. In business, loyalties are personal to the *bapak*, or boss, rather than to the organization itself. The term *bapak* (father) is indicative of the personal factor.

In these circumstances, not unknown elsewhere, it is easy to understand the development of patron/client relationships, whereby those with position, wealth, and prestige provide for the less fortunate and gain their loyalty in return, thus increasing their own prestige. It is a system open to nepotism, cronyism, and corruption, but strengthens the prestige and power of the patron and provides security and support for the client.

THE INDONESIAN CHINESE

Indonesian business and commerce owe a great deal to the input of the Indonesian Chinese. Their influence is immediately apparent in the commercial and business districts, where there are many Chinese premises and shops. In larger enterprises, the Chinese presence may not be so visible. Many Indonesians of Chinese origin have accepted Islam and adopted

Indonesian names. Moreover, many enterprises are joint enterprises between Chinese entrepreneurs and Indonesian partners.

The traditional Chinese social structure is based upon the patriarchal extended family. Chinese business structures throughout the region are often channeled through companies in which members of the extended family, settled elsewhere in the region as well as within Indonesia, have a controlling voice. Thus, the Chinese business structure is patterned on the family structure and based on kinship, loyalty, and subservience. Under a facade of modernization, these loyalties continue to affect decision making.

The combination of Indonesian family and patron/client relations on the one hand, and Chinese kinship loyalties on the other, require the exercise of caution. The person you are dealing with may be the front man for the real source of power, who may be, for example, a patriarch who does not even hold a formal position within the company. Treat contacts with courtesy and patience, for you too are being assessed.

OFFICE ETIQUETTE AND PROTOCOL

Expatriates, whether in management or not, must remember that they are regarded by their Indonesian colleagues as guests. Indonesian business relations are hierarchical and this should be recognized. In all dealings within the office it is important to maintain harmony of feelings. Thus it is necessary to learn about your staff as quickly as possible and to develop a sympathetic relationship with them. Making demands, issuing orders, publicly criticizing or humiliating staff, adopting an attitude of superiority, or professing greater knowledge and skills will be counterproductive. Indonesians respond positively to those who show an interest in them and their families, demonstrate curiosity about their culture and a desire to learn the language, and show a willingness to eat their food and accept their hospitality. Within the office, recognize the hierarchy of responsibilities and tasks and treat everyone with respect.

HIDDEN STATUS

Bear in mind that a person who may be in a low-status position in your office, perhaps a filing clerk or cleaner, may be of high status in his or her own community, perhaps on grounds of age or being a member of a traditional elite. Indonesians will recognize that status and will expect you to do so as well. This does not involve giving the person privileges, but merely addressing him or her correctly.

Authority and Face

At no point should a person be publicly reprimanded or criticized. Remember that the boss is called *bapak* and that Indonesians regard him, ideally, as a father figure. If the *bapak* discusses matters with an employee, whether management or worker, the latter is in the role of a child and if praised or consulted will feel encouraged to give of his or her best. If the *bapak* shows disappointment or disapproval, the employee will feel as if reprimanded by a father  and desire to improve. On the other hand, the relationship also expects that the subordinate will answer any summons and respond to any request. This arrangement operates throughout all levels of management, and just as a child will be upset and hurt by the anger of a father, so a subordinate will be greatly affected by the behavior of a superior who shouts and is abusive.

This desire to please can create problems in that subordinates may fail to pass on criticism or bad news to their superiors. There will be a tendency to tell you what they think you want to hear. Thus failings and problems will not be mentioned as early as they should. The way to counter this tendency is to rely on a trusted intermediary to ascertain the facts privately and thus provide accurate information in a way that does not embarrass or make *malu* (lose face) those subordinates involved.

Don't forget that, in your own office, *you* will be the *bapak*.

At some time expatriates will have dealings with government officials and civil servants. Many of these will be handled by intermediaries, but if you have personal contact with officials, remember that these are persons of status in Indonesian society and should be treated with courtesy and respect.

A Point of Etiquette
When presenting your business card, remember to do so with both hands, to show respect.

MANAGEMENT STYLE
It is clear from the above that management style should not be confrontational. Such an approach will only create disharmony, loss of respect, and lack of cooperation. Senior staff's advice and opinions should be asked for. They know better than an incomer the ways things work. Change is not impossible to achieve, but it can only occur after trust and respect have been established and confidence won. Be prepared to listen to advice

from other expatriates with experience in the enterprise and the office.

Learn something of the hierarchies within the office and work through them. Indonesians make great use of intermediaries or facilitators, who perform some of the functions of a private secretary but may not necessarily be part of the business structure. Much informal negotiation goes on between such intermediaries behind the scenes so that when a high-level meeting is finally arranged the decisions have already been made and the atmosphere is relaxed. It is not unlike the negotiations that precede a meeting of heads of state at which a decision or agreement is announced. It is therefore necessary to become aware of the correct channels of communication to those whom you wish to access and deal with.

The Secretary
Perhaps the most important person in your office will be the secretary. She will probably have worked in the office some time, may have worked for more than one of your predecessors, and will have knowledge of all the office procedures and of the personalities and status of those with whom you will have dealings, and of their strengths and failings. This applies to competent secretaries anywhere, but in Indonesia the nuances of personal and business relations differ from those

of the West and a good secretary will help you avoid embarrassing social blunders. She will give her loyalty to you as the *bapak* and can be a useful intermediary during negotiations with another department or office, not in substantive terms, but in sounding out through the secretary of your counterpart the mood and feeling there.

Introducing Change

Younger colleagues and subordinates trained overseas will be likely to fall in with Western management styles more easily than older colleagues without such a background. On the other hand, the latter will probably have knowledge and understanding of, and links with, the bureaucracy and existing management systems. Their advice and experience should be treated with respect and any changes introduced with regard for their views and feelings.

SPEECHES AND PRESENTATIONS

Indonesians love meetings, speeches, and presentations. These are opportunities for them to mingle, make contacts, and conduct informal discussions. While this is similar to Western-style networking, it is concerned with establishing a wide set of connections and relationships going beyond mere business. Positions in social and business hierarchies are assessed and personal, family, and regional connections ascertained, which will influence whatever business or professional relations may be established.

Speeches and presentations are often a means of confirming existing hierarchies and status figures. The Westerner will notice immediately the use of full titles and status markers. The formalities are recognized whatever criticism of policy may be implied in the speeches given. No one must be seen to lose face in public and what takes place is based on a consensus previously arrived at. Presentations of a technical nature will convey information, but without criticizing or belittling the procedures, applications, and techniques formerly in use. Negotiation will have taken place between interested parties and their intermediaries beforehand and face-saving strategies will have been devised. While perhaps frustrating to Western executives, these strategies are more productive than confrontation.

MEETINGS AND NEGOTIATIONS

Indonesians enjoy meetings and one will see traditional and communal attitudes at work. In public life and business there is always a striving for consensus. Behind the scenes, trusted intermediaries will be at work producing compromises and solutions to which all parties can finally agree. Inevitably, this can result in issues being fudged or agreement that a situation will be reassessed after a period of time.

KEY WORDS AND CONCEPTS	
Gotong royong	mutual cooperation, working together
Muafakat	consensus, mutual agreement
Mesyuarat	discussion, mutual exchange of views and ideas, with respect for individual feelings and avoidance of loss of face

BUREAUCRACY AND CORRUPTION

Indonesian bureaucracy exists to see that procedures are followed. Government officials regard themselves as persons with authority and expect to be treated with respect. They may be civil, but they are not your servants. Be respectful, defer to their advice and to the procedures in place, and you will be courteously treated. To show irritation and impatience serves no purpose. Do not be tempted to offer favors in return for speedier service. While in some circumstances there may be short-term gain, you will lose their respect and acquire no long-term advantage.

Your Indonesian business associates will often have family or social links to local and national political elites and bureaucrats. The separation of interests is not always clear. Former politicians, civil servants, and military personnel are often connected with private and state business enterprises. The existence of patron/client networks adds another potential for the dispensation of favors. It is best to be aware of these connections, but to confine your business dealings to your actual or prospective business partners.

Because of the emphasis placed on personal dealings in business relations, it is important to check out the credentials of prospective business partners and their companies. Be wary of those who provide lavish hospitality and gifts, placing you under an obligation, and then offer contacts and information at a price. If offered hospitality or gifts, reciprocate to an equal degree, thus reestablishing your status.

GIFT GIVING

The giving and receiving of gifts is a delicate matter and each situation has to be assessed on its merits. Generally, hospitality and gifts should be roughly matched. Sweets, flowers, and ornamental objects, particularly items from your own country, are appreciated. Be wary of giving or receiving expensive items like jewelry. Remember that gifts of alcohol are inappropriate for a Muslim and any gifts of food should be *halal*. It is advisable to be aware of the religious affiliations and possible sensitivities of all potential recipients. This is an area in which the advice of an experienced secretary or personal assistant can be invaluable.

Establishing Status

A European businessman, negotiating with a group of Indonesian businessmen in a town away from where he worked, had been invited by them to an elaborate meal at a good restaurant.

Before the next and final meeting, to be hosted by him, he provided for the visiting Indonesian delegation to dine at a prestigious restaurant near his place of business, carefully selecting the menu in advance to make sure that the finest delicacies were available.

At the negotiations the following day, he obtained most of what he desired, and is convinced that by reciprocating their hospitality with perhaps slightly superior hospitality he substantially improved his bargaining position, so that muafakat *was quickly reached. He, too, had compromised on some issues, but face had been saved all around and each side was content with the outcome.*

WOMEN IN BUSINESS

Women in Indonesia enjoy relatively high status, which may differ between the different Indonesian cultures. They are active in smaller family businesses, and the educated are to be found across the professions. In larger businesses and corporate enterprises they are increasingly evident, mainly in secretarial and clerical roles, but  also in management. Middle and higher management remains male dominated. Nevertheless, women are in a position to act as intermediaries between their expatriate colleagues and superiors, as noted previously with regard to the role of the secretary. Expatriate women employed at the managerial level may find their position awkward as the culture remains male oriented, a situation familiar also in the West. An expatriate woman may find herself sidelined and bypassed, but not subject to aggressive or unpleasant behavior. As in any situation in Indonesia, the answer is to work within the established hierarchical and patron/client relationships and establish one's own network of contacts.

Expatriate men should show courtesy and respect to their female staff, many of whom will have the knowledge, contacts, and skills to ease their path. Indonesian culture is conservative, and brash, rude behavior will be regarded as insulting.

WORKING WITHIN THE SYSTEM

Working in Indonesia requires patience and understanding of the traditions and mores of Indonesian society, which affect relations in the workplace. Enough has been said above to indicate the pitfalls. Indonesian business practices can readily be seen as, and often are, prone to corruption and nepotism as well as to procrastination and delay. The temptation may be to fall in with this perceived pattern of behavior. This can be self-defeating, as can be the temptation to rage against the system. An outsider, however, has some advantages in not being tied in to any faction and has his or her own cards to play: to build up one's own networks independently, to acquire trustworthy intermediaries prepared to represent and further your views and interests, and to work within the system and influence the main players in it.

chapter **eight**

COMMUNICATING

LANGUAGES

More than five hundred languages are spoken, but Bahasa Indonesia is the national language taught in schools and spoken in all but the remotest areas. English is widely spoken in the main tourist areas and in business and commercial organizations. Indonesian office employees and colleagues with whom you work will have a good grasp of English and will switch from one language to the other in the course of conversation among themselves.

Lower-ranking and service staff may have limited English. It is advisable to learn conversational Indonesian, both as a matter of courtesy and as a means of placing Indonesians at their ease with you. It will please them that you make the effort to learn and use their language. It also enables you to keep abreast of office gossip and be aware of what may be going on. In time you will find yourself speaking an international *patois*, lacing your sentences with Indonesian words and phrases.

Language in the Media

There is a very active Indonesian media scene and ready access also to English-language media, particularly in Jakarta. The *Jakarta Post* is an English-language newspaper that provides very good coverage of world and Indonesian news. News and commentary is focused more on Asia and Australasia than Europe, but international editions of foreign newspapers are also available. Cable and satellite television provide access to the outside world and radio broadcasts in English can be received from Radio Australia, BBC World Service, Voice of America, and other providers.

SPEAKING BAHASA INDONESIA

The national language, Bahasa Indonesia, is a standardized Malay almost identical to that adopted by Malaysia, Singapore, and Brunei. Given the history of the archipelago, the language has taken words from a variety of sources— Sanskrit, Arabic, Chinese, Portuguese, Dutch, and English. Pronunciation presents few problems for English speakers and it is relatively easy to acquire a working vocabulary. The written form has been romanized and is easy to read.

Although English is the language of business and tourism and Indonesians will want to practice their English with you, they are delighted when visitors use their language, even if only the basic greetings and courtesies. Moreover, English speakers are rare outside the tourist and business center and there may be times when some knowledge of the language is very useful. You will notice that a number of words in current use are familiar, having been taken from English and given an Indonesian spelling.

The notes on pronunciation on page 163 are a guide to speaking and understanding standard Bahasa Indonesia. In practice you will discover that there are regional variations in pronunciation and considerable elision, which makes understanding what is said difficult—but these same problems are found in English-speaking countries as well. Most people will happily slow their speech and standardize their pronunciation when they realize your difficulty. More importantly, they will respect you for trying.

Learning Indonesian

If you are going to Indonesia to work, your employers may provide Indonesian classes. If not, and if you are staying for some time, ask around for a class or a teacher. You may be in an English-speaking environment, but some knowledge of the language, however simple, can greatly increase your enjoyment and open up opportunities to learn more about the country and the people. Formal

Indonesian has structures and forms, including prefixes and suffixes, that are difficult to grasp, but you can get by with a basic knowledge. In this sense, it has some of the characteristics of English.

FACE-TO-FACE

As we have seen, people should be addressed with the respect that their position calls for and the courtesies maintained. Face should be saved and no public humiliation imposed. Be aware that you will often be told what your interlocutor believes you want to hear. Pay attention to nuances of behavior and tone. The true situation may only be revealed through intermediaries.

Malu

Indonesians will refer to feeling *malu*, a sense of shame, embarrassment, and loss of face. It implies that the person has suffered a loss of status and has been belittled. There is no single English word to cover its connotations for the Indonesian, for whom it represents a loss of a sense of self-worth. It can be brought about by small actions. Persons may feel *malu* because of a fault or minor act of disrespect of their own as well as by a reprimand or criticism leveled at them.

Western-trained Indonesians may be forthcoming in private, but unwilling to state their views openly. Remember that even Western-educated Indonesians may not understand all the subtleties of the English words they speak; just as you will be unaware of those of Indonesian. Be prepared to ask in tactful ways for information to be re-presented. Do not show irritation or anger if matters are misunderstood. Attempt to improve your own presentation and always try to keep the atmosphere calm. It may be necessary to employ a third person to act as an interpreter, not of the words themselves but of their meaning and implication.

Joining In

Karaoke has caught on in Indonesia. At office functions or evenings out be prepared to sing along. It is not necessary, but it may do more for relations with your staff than any other single gesture.

HUMOR

Indonesians have a well developed sense of humor. The traditional drama of the region encompasses elements of slapstick and coarse comedy that enliven the more uplifting stories of divine beings, kings, and heroes. In a society in which status is important, the pretensions of the social upstart are a source of humor. There is also a tradition of verbal humor, which will remain opaque until the visitor learns the language.

There is, however, a fine line between what is humorous and what produces shame. An Indonesian to whom you are speaking may laugh to cover embarrassment, perhaps because he or she has lost track of what you are saying. If that appears to be the case, rephrase what you have said. On the other hand, as a foreigner, you will make mistakes and have experiences that are funny. Your Indonesian acquaintances will be too polite to laugh outright but, if you show that you can laugh at yourself, they will be delighted that you are not overcome by embarrassment and will join in.

NONVERBAL COMMUNICATION

One's body language is as important as the spoken word. Indonesians will smile and nod, not necessarily because they understand, but because it is polite to do so. On being greeted a person may hold your hand for longer than you wish. Do not snatch it away. Be careful with your gestures. Use the whole hand or the thumb to point, not the index finger. Be aware of how you stand and sit so that you do not give out wrong messages. Read again the advice on social behavior in Chapter 2.

GESTURES AND BODY LANGUAGE

One can give offense without meaning to.
Gestures we use automatically may in other
cultures be discourteous. While Indonesians are
polite enough to make allowances for
foreigners, the following points may help you
avoid embarrassment for yourself and for them.

- When giving or receiving something,
  never use your left hand, which is
  considered unclean. In a more formal
  situation, support your right hand at
  the elbow with the left hand and bow
  slightly. To offer a gift, present it with
  both hands.

- Beckoning with an upturned palm or
  with a finger is considered vulgar. To
  summon someone, use your right hand
  with the palm downward and make a
  motion toward yourself with the wrist.

- Do not point with your first finger. Use
  your thumb or your right palm turned
  upward. In some places outside Java the
  finger is acceptable, but avoid pointing
  directly at a person. Never use your foot.

- Avoid touching an adult or child on the head, which is considered sacred. If it is necessary to touch a person's head, ask permission first. Paradoxically, Indonesians are often unable to resist touching the head of a fair-haired child.

- Stand relaxed with your hands clasped either in front or behind. Do not put your hands in your pockets. Do not lean against a wall. Never stand with your hands on your hips, as this is a sign of aggression.

- Sit up straight. Do not put your hands behind your head. If crossing your legs, do not point your foot at anyone. On the floor, men should sit with their legs crossed, women with their legs drawn to one side.

- When introduced to an Indonesian, shake hands with a light grip, giving your name. Many Indonesians, especially Muslims, may raise the right hand toward the heart. A greeting may be emphasized by clasping the offered hand with two hands and bringing both toward the chest.

- When men and women meet, the woman may extend her hand to be taken lightly for a moment. If the woman does not extend her hand, the man should give a slight nod.

- Remove your shoes when entering a private house and if visiting a mosque.

- When passing in front of a group of seated people, you should stoop a little, extend the right hand toward the ground and make your way past as unobtrusively as possible.

- If you need to blow your nose, move away to do so. Most Indonesians find the idea of blowing your nose into a handkerchief, which you then put in your pocket or purse, revolting.

- Indonesians have a different sense of private space and you should not be alarmed or offended by people sitting close to you or touching you. Except among the more daring young people, persons of the opposite sex usually avoid touching, but those of the same sex touch a great deal.

- Public displays of affection between persons of the opposite sex are not acceptable.

Observe the behavior of your Indonesian hosts and companions. If in doubt, be courteous, self-effacing, and restrained. Once Indonesians accept you as a friend, then, in their company, formality may be relaxed. By then, also, without really noticing it, you will be observing Indonesian etiquette.

MEANS OF COMMUNICATION
Telephone
Service is good in Jakarta and the larger cities, and the international service is fine. Cell phones are rapidly replacing landlines in personal communication. There were 30 million in use in 2004, up from 11.7 million in 2002, and the trend continues.

E-mail
The Internet is increasingly used in business and private communications, but it is advisable to retain hard copies in case of problems. There were 18 million Internet users in 2005, up from 8 million in 2002. Services are less reliable outside Jakarta. The Internet country code for Indonesia is .id.

Postal Service
The postal service is not particularly reliable. Business and commerce rely largely on private couriers or their own courier systems.

THE MEDIA
There has been an increase in freedom of the media since the fall of President Suharto and the closing of the Ministry of Information, which controlled domestic media and restricted access to foreign media.

The Press

The two main mass-circulation dailies in Bahasa Indonesia are *Kompass* and *Pos Kota*.

There is a wide range of printed media in Bahasa Indonesia and foreign newspapers in English are available in Jakarta and larger centers, particularly in hotel gift shops and other outlets catering to foreigners. The English language daily newspaper is the *Jakarta Post*.

Radio

Radio Republik Indonesia (PRI) is the public broadcaster, operating six national networks, regional and local stations, and the external service Voice of Indonesia.

There are a large number of private radio stations throughout the country, which supply news and music.

Foreign broadcasters like the Voice of America, the BBC World Service, and Radio Australia can be accessed.

Television

The public television service, Televisi Republik Indonesia (TVRI), operates two networks.

There are some ten national commercial networks, including SCTV, RCTI, TPI, and Metro TV. Some provinces operate their own stations.

News Agency
The government news agency, Antara, has
English-language pages.

CONCLUSION

Indonesia is a vast, diverse, and fascinating country
with friendly, hospitable people. Despite this
diversity, its many ethnic groups share a core Asian
approach to the world. They place great emphasis
on status, respect for elders and superiors, and
socially correct behavior. They seek to avoid
confrontation and to maintain harmony and
consensus, and are highly sensitive to criticism and
to loss of face. In this book we have sought to equip
you to develop good relationships with those
Indonesians you meet, so that your stay in the
country will be positive and mutually rewarding.

Appendix 1: Pronunciation

Consonants are as in English, with these exceptions:

b	at the end of a word, like "p" in "gap"
c	like "ch" in "church"
d	at the end of a word, like "t" in "hat"
f	pronounced as in "fat," but often replaced by "p"
g	always hard, as in "get"
h	between two different vowels, pronounced lightly or not at all: *tahu* (know)—tau
k	at the end of words, like a glottal stop: *tidak* (not/no)—tida'
kh	like "ch" in "loch"
ng	as in "singer"
ngg	as in "linger"
ny	as in "bunion"
sy	like "sh" in "ship": *syarikat* (a company)—sharikat

Vowels in open syllables are pronounced differently from those in closed syllables:

a	open syllables, like "u" in "up": *apa* (where)
	closed syllables, slightly shorter: *makan* (to eat)—mahkan
e	when unstressed, as in "open"
	when stressed, as in "bed"
i	open syllables, like "ee"
	closed syllables, as in "hit"
o	open syllables, as in "open"
	closed syllables, as in "hot"
u	open syllables, as in "oo" in "boot"
	closed syllables, as in "cut"

Diphthongs are pronounced as follows:

ai	open syllables, like "i" in "kite": *pantai* (beach)
	closed syllables, pronounced as two separate sounds a – i: *baik* (well/good)—ba-eek
au	open syllables, like "ow" in "how"
	closed syllables, two separate sounds ow-u: *laut* (sea)

Appendix 2: Useful Phrases

Greetings

Good morning (up to 11:00 a.m.)	*Selamat pagi*
Good day (11:00 a.m. to 3:00 p.m.)	*Selamat siang*
Good afternoon	*Selamat sore*
Good evening/good night	*Selamat malam*

One may also be greeted with "*Halo*" and "*Hai*" (Hello and Hi) by the young and Westernized.

Welcome	*Selamat datang*
How are you?	*Apa kabar?*
Well/fine	*Baik*
Fine, and how are you?	*Baik: dan apa kabat saudara?*
Good-bye (to person leaving)	*Selamat jalan*
Good-bye (to person remaining behind)	*Selamat tinggal*
See you later	*Sampai jumpa lagi*

Polite Phrases

Please	*Tolong*
Thank you (very much)	*Terimah kasih* (*banyak*)
Very good	*Baik kesali*
Please do	*Silakan*
You're welcome	*Kembali*
Excuse me/sorry/pardon	*Maaf*
It doesn't matter	*Tidak apa*
It's OK	*Boleh*
No/not	*Tidak*
Yes	*Ya*

Forms of Address

Indonesians will address each other (and you) using titles of respect. *Bapak* (or *Pak*) and *Ibu* (or *Bu*) are polite ways to address older men or women or officials

Sir	*Tuan* (usually for foreigners)
Madam	*Nonya*
Miss	*Nona*
Mr.	*Pak, Tuan*
Mrs.	*Bu, Nyonya*

A man who has made the pilgrimage to Mecca is addressed as *Haji*, a woman who has made the pilgrimage as *Hajjah*.

Further Reading

Bresban, John. *Managing Indonesia; The Modern Political Economy*. New York: Colombia University Press, 1993.

Legge, J. D. *Sukarno: A Political Biography*. Harmondsworth: Penguin, 1973.

MacIntyre, Ian. *Business and Politics in Indonesia*. Sydney: Allen & Unwin, 1991.

May, Brian. *The Indonesian Tragedy*. London: Routledge & Kegan Paul, 1978; and in paperback, Singapore: Graham Brash.

This is a history of Indonesia from independence that attempts to understand its problems and difficulties.

Polomka, Peter. *Indonesia Since Sukarno*. Harmondsworth: Penguin, 1971.

For an introduction to the history, cultures, and arts of Indonesia see two series produced by Oxford University Press in Singapore and Kuala Lumpur in the 1980s and 1990s. The series, Oxford in Asia Paperbacks, includes reprints of nineteenth- and twentieth-century accounts of the region. The following titles are still in print:

Java

de Wit, Augusta. *Java. Facts and Fancies.*

Dumarcy, Jacques. *The Temples of Java* (he has also written on Borobudur).

Poortenaar, Jan. *An Artist in Java.*

Russ, James R. *Java: A Traveller's Anthology.*

Scidmore, E. R. *Java: The Gardens of the East.*

Smythies, Michael. *Yogyakarta: Cultural Heart of Indonesia.*

Sumatra

Schnitger, F. M. *Forgotten Kingdoms in Sumatra.*

Reid, Anthony. *Witnesses to Sumatra.*

Bali

Covarrubias, Miguel. *Island of Bali.*

Powell, Hickman. *The Last Paradise.*

Vickers, Adrian. *Travelling in Bali: Four Hundred Years of Journeys.*

Kalimantan

Lumholtz, Karl. *Through Central Borneo.*

General

Collins, G.E.P. *Makassar Sailing.*

Forbes, Anna. *Unbeaten Tracks in the Islands of the Far East.*

Miller, George. *To the Spice Islands and Beyond: Travels in Eastern Indonesia.*

For those interested in Indonesian culture, the Oxford in Asia series Images in Asia includes the following titles:

Djelantik, A. A. M. *Balinese Paintings.*

Lu, Sylvia Fraser. *Indonesian Batik: Processes, Patterns and Places.*

Smithies, Michael. *Yogyakarta: Cultural Heart of Indonesia.*

van Deek, Aart. *Life in the Javanese Kraton.*

culture smart! **indonesia**

Index

Acknowledgments

I would like to dedicate this book to Robert and Lennaa.

Thanks to Gordon and Margaret Beedham for permission to use their recent photographs, and Carole Beedham and Mat Parkin for information on expatriate life in Jakarta.